The Constructivist Credo

We all live every day in a virtual environment,
defined by our ideas

—Michael Crichton, in *Disclosure*

The Constructivist Credo

Yvonna S. Lincoln
Egon G. Guba

Walnut Creek, California

LEFT COAST PRESS, INC.
1630 North Main Street, #400
Walnut Creek, CA 94596
http://www.LCoastPress.com

Left Coast Press, Inc. is committed to preserving ancient forests and natural resources. We elected to print this title on 30% post consumer recycled paper, processed chlorine free. As a result, for this printing, we have saved:

3 Trees (40' tall and 6-8" diameter)
1 Million BTUs of Total Energy
249 Pounds of Greenhouse Gases
1,349 Gallons of Wastewater
91 Pounds of Solid Waste

Left Coast Press, Inc. made this paper choice because our printer, Thomson-Shore, Inc., is a member of Green Press Initiative, a nonprofit program dedicated to supporting authors, publishers, and suppliers in their efforts to reduce their use of fiber obtained from endangered forests.

For more information, visit www.greenpressinitiative.org

Environmental impact estimates were made using the Environmental Defense Paper Calculator. For more information visit: www.papercalculator.org.

ISBN 978-1-59874-689-1 hardcover
ISBN 978-1-59874-690-7 paperback
978-1-59874-691-4 institutional eBook
ISBN 978-1-61132-461-7 consumer eBook

Library of Congress Cataloging-in-Publication Data

Lincoln, Yvonna S.
  The constructivist credo / Yvonna S. Lincoln, Egon G. Guba.
    pages cm
  Includes bibliographical references.
  ISBN 978-1-59874-689-1 (hardback : alk. paper)—ISBN 978-1-59874-690-7 (pbk. : alk. paper)—ISBN 978-1-59874-691-4 (institutional ebook)—ISBN 978-1-61132-461-7 (consumer ebook)
  1. Social sciences—Research—Philosophy. 2. Constructivism (Philosophy) 3. Constructivism (Psychology) I. Guba, Egon G. II. Title.
  H62.L4826 2013
  300.72—dc23
                    2013009000

Printed in the United States of America

    The paper used in this publication meets the minimum requirements of American National Standard for Information Sciences—Permanence of Paper for Printed Library Materials, ANSI/NISO Z39.48–1992.

Contents

Introduction

Yvonna S. Lincoln

This little work is the result of a thirteen-year "conversation" between my late husband and myself, over dinner, over breakfast, over coffee, between bouts of pleasure reading and professional reading. It was born during a period of time when I ran an informal seminar at our house. These seminars, where my students met once a month to review pieces of each other's proposals and dissertations, were the fodder of long and complex discussions. One student would volunteer (a term I use loosely, since some were assigned) to bring in the next step of her or his proposal or dissertation: a problem statement, a literature review, a methodology chapter, a findings chapter, or an implications chapter. The volunteer would make certain everyone in the group got a copy of the material at least two weeks in advance, and each student (usually only six or eight students in the group at a time) would prepare critical comments on the work, designed to enable the presenter to refine his or her work, to consider questions that had not yet been raised, to clarify sections that might appear murky or obscure, or to push the presenter to think more deeply about some section. The group not only contributed substantive issues, they were encouraged to provide editorial advice also, a process

The Constructivist Credo, by Yvonna S. Lincoln and Egon G. Guba. 7–13
© 2013 Left Coast Press, Inc. All rights reserved.

that improved not only the presenter's work, but which also improved, over time, their own writing.

I ran these seminars not only at Texas A&M, but also at the University of Kansas and at Vanderbilt University. They proved highly efficient for me, since I could work with multiple students at one time. More importantly, however, I believe they proved highly effective for the students. They clearly were developing their critical abilities, they had a faithful "writing group," and they taught each other in rich and rewarding ways. Some of the individuals from the original dissertation "seminars" (no credit was ever offered) still maintain contact with each other, and still pass along their own papers and chapters requesting comments and criticisms. In short, some built colleagueships that have lasted a lifetime. To make the sessions more invitational, someone was also charged each week with bringing a dessert, and I made coffee and tea, which we shared at the end of the session.

During the early years, Egon was, of course, not able to attend many of the seminars, since he had students, courses, and university work of his own. But after his retirement, both during the Vanderbilt years and here at Texas A&M, he often sat in on the seminars and worked alongside the students, offering his own comments and critical analyses. It was during those sessions, and particularly with those students deep into their dissertations, who came with serious methodological questions prompted by their own fieldwork, that this book came into existence.

Egon and I frequently made notes on the students' questions, and we didn't always have the answers. Frequently, students would proffer solutions, some of which we avidly considered and borrowed. Egon, however, retired and, with a still-active mind, determined that we should keep some record of our thinking and the kinds of answers we worked out either in the presence of the students or after they had gone. Other times, the "solutions" were developed in the hundreds of conversations between us. Egon took it upon himself to begin typing up the conundra and the solutions we recognized, adopted, or adapted from our own reasoning or that of the students. He would write a section, I would read it the next day, and we would talk about it, make notes about revisions, extend some thought, or begin a new line of propositions. For years, I carried pieces of this work onto airplanes with me, since that is quiet time, with no phones, no one knocking at the office door, and no e-mail demanding attention!

The first "Credo" was just three pages long, and Egon titled it "The Constructivists' Bible"! Over the next fifteen years, it grew into a document some 50 pages long, single-spaced. That document turned out, however, not to be the final document.

After his long illness, when I picked up the text again, I realized that both of us had matured, grown more sophisticated about the constructivists' project, read far more, and had generally moved beyond our first proposals. If this credo were going to be published, it would have to be edited, line by line, to bring it into some coherence, and to shape it to reflect our more current thinking. First, both of us had grown far more critical (by which I mean, critical theorist-leaning), no doubt influenced by Norman K. Denzin, my co-editor and co-author on *Qualitative Inquiry* and the four editions of the *SAGE Handbook of Qualitative Research,* as well as the *Handbook of Critical and Indigenous Methodologies;* by the virtual explosion of good critical theorist work; and by the contemporary political climate, right-leaning and hostile to anything qualitative. The second thing readers familiar with our earlier writing will notice is that the "conjectures" do not necessarily follow any order we have used in the past. That is, because the conjectures themselves frequently grew from questions posed to us, sometimes from our own consulting, or from our logical projections of what should be in the set, the work as it now stands has been updated—although Egon needs to accept no blame for that, as any mistakes, misunderstandings, or alterations are solely my own.

As a consequence of my own re-thinking of the original manuscript, I have come to realize that it bears many influences: a distinctly and decidedly political bent, recognizing, among others, the arguments of Patti Lather and Bettie St. Pierre (as well as many others); and a strong affiliation with the constructivist grounded theory work of Kathy Charmaz, whose boundary-pushing beyond the deductive and inductive into the abductive (2008) has proven useful again and again (see, for instance, B6 in the Credo, where our thinking began to foreshadow what Kathy helped to make clear to us). Among other characteristics are a willingness to begin to see constructivist inquiry as a means to open up the hidden in social life and thereby begin to extend the possibilities for an extended social justice and create some opportunities for what Westwood called "navigating the contemporary"—exposing the linkages between seemingly unrelated social phenomena—in order to begin to think about whether this is the world we wanted to create (2008; see also Lincoln & Guba, 2011), and if not, what would be our alternative proposal. In fact, the influences are likely too numerous to name, simply because we can rarely recognize in ourselves when our own thinking began to change, or who it was we read a week ago that jolted us sufficiently to begin the change process. A journal article, a chapter, a paper at a conference, a casual conversation across lunch or dinner: all shift us immeasurably and ultimately untrackably. We simply wake up some morning and discover that our thinking has changed.

Even so, this manuscript likely does not represent everything I would teach my students today about constructivist inquiry or the inquiry process more broadly. Because my own classes are highly diverse, I now talk far more extensively about what I term the "lenses" through which we filter research findings: feminist theory (in its manifold forms); racial and ethnic theories; the variety of critical theories, including Latino critical studies; border theories; neo-colonial theories; hybridity theories; diaspora theories; and queer theories, among others. These lenses represent major new theoretical underpinnings for what is disparagingly termed "identity politics" but which is more usefully and significantly thought of as theoretical approaches to understanding the subtleties and nuances of difference—cultural, social, political, national, race-based, gender-based, and the like—and giving up, once and for all, the idea of a "melting pot" where all come to share precisely the same epistemological standpoint (which is now understood to be white, male, European, Western canon-derivative). Nor does the book deal, in any meaningful way, with the problems and issues of "researching up," or confronting and obtaining information from powerful and well-funded elites. Elites, particularly those who do not share our own political leanings (whatever those may be), frequently do not wish to engage our projects in any meaningful way and are in a perfect position to resist the best blandishments of an ardent social science.

It also has not dealt with a foundational issue we are beginning to understand today: that we may not, in fact, learn what there is to know, that there will always remain hidden from us as social scientists, information which others do not wish us to have, and which they are well-positioned to keep from us (Faubion & Marcus, 2009; Westbrook, 2008). Furthermore, the "linkages" which connect various power nexuses to one another may, despite our best efforts, not be visible to us, even with the most assiduous and careful fieldwork (Westbrook, 2008).

What this work does do is to tease out some more subtle "conjectures" about how constructivism works, and how a constructivist might conduct herself when confronted with a variety of possibilities in the field.

Consequently, there is a brief section (Part 1) which deals with the presumptions or assumptions that constructivists are likely to make in the pursuit of their work. While we originally worked with ontology, epistemology, and methodology, I have extended the work to include axiology, or the role of values in human inquiry (and edited to try to capture that extension of thinking, since we both deemed it crucial to ensure that values were an integral part of the constructivist paradigm and not set outside it, as values appear to be in positivist models of inquiry). I have also edited Egon's "Aim and Hope" statement to reflect four rather than three presumptions, since the L1–L7 "Conjectures" deal with both politics and ethics, and consequently with values as they enter into the inquiry process.

We originally tried to indicate some beginning conjectures (A1–A11), which represent assumptions that are likely to be a part of the worldview of those who are persuaded to constructivism in an *a priori* way. In some of these conjectures, other scholars have led the way (for instance, Elliott Eisner and Karl Weick), and we utilized their formulations throughout, since the work of other scholars had been foundational in shaping our own thinking. Sections 2B and 2C concern themselves with the nature of constructions, both individual and social (shared), and how we as human beings mediate the world with our own and with shared construals about meaning. It was our hope here to help readers understand that "reality" exists in two forms: physical reality—the "stuff" about which positivists are frequently concerned—and socially constructed realities, or the meaning-making activities and meaning-ascribed realities on which people are far more likely to act and respond. While constructivists would never deny that each of us must navigate a physical reality (How many students are signed up for our class this semester? What kind of electronic and technical support features are in that classroom which will help us to utilize technology most effectively in the teaching-learning process? How many actual dollars will support graduate assistantships this year?), constructivists recognize that it is rarely the raw physical reality which shapes our behavior and our response to the physical environment. It is, rather, the meanings we associate with any given tangible reality or social interaction which determines how we respond.

Section 2D revolves about the nature of knowledge, how knowledge comes about, and the search for empirical verification. Section 2E deals with dependence and voice, by which is meant the dependence of "facts" on prior constructions (frequently, what we as a community of scientists can come to agree are facts), and with the role of voice as the communicator of constructions and the values which undergird those constructions. Section 2F is a set of reflections on the nature of paradigms and the kinds we carry around with us. Section 2G recaps some of our earlier work, some of which is written down nowhere until now. We struggled with this segment originally because, although many of our students announced that they wanted careers in teaching and research, they seemed to have thought little about what "research" or inquiry was in any systematic way.

Section 2H expands upon what we had already written regarding hermeneutic and dialectic methodology, or research strategy. It reinforces the point which we and many other thoughtful researchers and authors have made—namely, that not all research strategies are useful for all paradigms of inquiry. In fact, some may be, we argued, dysfunctional. The following section, 2I, examines quality criteria for constructivist inquiry, especially since quality criteria are different for each paradigm—what may make sense for experimental inquiry is virtually useless for constructivist inquiry, and vice versa. Section 2J takes up the issue of application, and how broadly findings may be applicable beyond the local context. Section 2K is a brief treatise on change and the possibility of change in the face of reified constructions. Here the critical theorists would find themselves right at home, since they are frequently concerned with "truths" defined in an *a priori* way, especially some reified truth which benefits one class of individuals while seriously disadvantaging another.

Section 2L takes up the contested arena of ethics and politics. While it is clear that the Belmont Report's standards for ethics do not go nearly far enough in the protection and affordance of dignity to research participants, we are not finally decided on a firm and standardized code of ethics for a constructivist—or any other qualitative, ethnographic, or interpretive—form of inquiry. Consequently, ethics, as well as the ongoing politics of constructivist work, will continue to be debated. Section 2M deals with case studies—case reports of research—and some guidelines for what they should look like, what they should contain, and what kinds of knowledge will generally be useful to multiple stakeholding audiences.

A brief case study is included to demonstrate how some of these theses get worked out in the practice of research. I selected the dissertation of a recent PhD, Elaine Demps, and tried to show how different constructivist principles informed, and were used within, her work. Finally, there is a brief statement, written by Egon, but enlarged by me, regarding what he and I believed to be the missions of a research university from the perspective of a constructivist.

Acknowledgment

I wish to gratefully acknowledge the permission granted by Dr. Elaine L. Demps for the use of her dissertation chapters as exemplars of how some of the presumptions get worked out.

References

Charmaz, K. (2008). Grounded theory as an emergent method. In S. N. Hesse-Biber & P. Leavy (Eds.), *Handbook of emergent methods* (pp. 155–172). New York: Guilford Press.

Demps, E. L. (2008). *Understanding the faculty experience of teaching using educational technology at public research universities in the academic capitalism era: An interpretive critical inquiry.* Unpublished dissertation. College Station: Texas A&M University.

Faubion, J. D. & Marcus, G. E. (Eds.). (2009). *Fieldwork is not what it used to be: Learning anthropology's method in a time of transition.* Ithaca, NY: Cornell University Press.

Westbrook, D. A. (2008). *Navigators of the contemporary: Why ethnography matters.* Chicago: University of Chicago Press.

Egon Guba

Observations on a Journey to Constructivism

Thomas A. Schwandt

Scholar-teachers do not simply know, they profess. Those who are exceptional at professing do more than convey reasoned, coherent, and thoughtful justifications for their ideas. The best professors are characteristically open to revising what they profess and even abandoning once strongly held positions in light of new knowledge gained through practical experience, conversations with colleagues, and in consideration of the scholarly work of others. Egon's intellectual journey was characterized by this combination of traits and dispositions.

In the thirty years that I knew him, first as a student then as a colleague, we had many exchanges in person and via correspondence about our respective views on the methodology and epistemology of qualitative inquiry, the idea of research paradigms, and theories of evaluation. We debated ideas and offered justifications for our positions, yet I never directly inquired how he came to hold the views that he held. To fully explain the genesis or, perhaps better said, the evolution of his commitment to constructivist philosophy remains an unfinished task awaiting the skills of a biographer, which I am not. Yet, my hope is that what follows conveys something of what it was like for Egon to profess. Perhaps

The Constructivist Credo, by Yvonna S. Lincoln and Egon G. Guba. 15–24

by having some sense of his scholarly temperament readers may better appreciate how he came to the intellectual commitments for which he is best known.

Egon was thoroughly prepared as a quantitative methodologist, having completed a bachelor's degree in Mathematics and Physics (Valparaiso University, 1947); a master's in Statistics and Measurement (University of Kansas, 1950); and a PhD in Statistics (University of Chicago, 1952). After five years as an Assistant Professor of Education at the University of Chicago, Egon held a brief appointment (1957–58) as Associate Professor of Education at the University of Kansas City (now the University of Missouri at Kansas City) and then spent eight years at the Ohio State University (1958–66), followed by twenty-three years at Indiana University, Bloomington, where he retired in 1989.

The period from roughly the mid-1950s through the late 1960s was a time of rapid expansion of federal interest and investment in the educational research and development (R&D) enterprise—not simply in terms of new funding for sponsored projects but also in terms of the significant growth of programs for the preparation of educational researchers at the doctoral level. During this time, as Clark Kerr (1963) explains in *The Uses of the University,* some fifty to one hundred universities sought to position themselves as "Federal Grant Universities"— those who aspired to be among the top recipients of federal research contracts, had developed specialized research institutes, and received 30 or more percent of their income from federal contracts. Although investments in research in the behavioral and natural sciences may have drawn the most attention during this time, similar aspirations to establish the educational research enterprise were quite evident, not least in large major public universities like Ohio State.

Egon's early career unfolded in this heady period of expansion of educational R&D. In the eight years he was on the faculty at Ohio State University he was, successively, head of the Division of Educational Research in the Bureau of Educational Research and Service; coordinator of research in the College of Education; and director of the Bureau of Educational Research and Service (while in that role in 1963 he established an evaluation center in the Bureau and hired Daniel Stufflebeam to direct it). When he moved to Indiana University in 1966, Egon continued for several years to serve roles in the R&D enterprise as director of the National Institute for the Study of Educational Change; associate dean for Academic Affairs; and co-director of the Research on Institutions of Teacher Education (RITE) Project.

In the mid- to late-1960s, there was growing optimism among many educational researchers and practitioners that the federal government would be able to fund large efforts aimed at school improvement. There was widespread belief in the idea that innovations could be developed outside of actual educational settings (**R**esearch), given trials in certain school sites (**D**evelopment), and then, eventually, become widely disseminated (**Di**ffusion), resulting in a significant system level change in educational practices (Thomas, 1975).

It was against this backdrop that Egon's work during these years was focused on the development of R, D, & D models for federal policies for educational research that would, in turn, effect significant improvement-oriented change in educational practice. In 1965, along with his colleague David Clark at Indiana University, he published a paper on change process theory that became widely known as the Clark-Guba model for educational research, development, and diffusion that reflected this growing optimism (Clark & Guba, 1965). Ten years later, in response to criticisms surrounding the theoretical and empirical adequacy of that model, they abandoned it and developed the configurational perspective of knowledge production and utilization (Guba & Clark, 1975). This disposition to revise and reconsider earlier views (see also Clark & Guba, 1972)—perhaps first evident in the way in which he and Clark revised their initial R, D, & D model—would come to characterize Egon's continued conceptualizations of evaluation and educational research as his ideas about the methodology of naturalistic inquiry evolved.

It was also in the mid-1960s that the theory and practice of program evaluation in education began to develop as mandates to evaluate were incorporated into federally funded education and social programs. At its outset, experimentalists and psychometricians dominated the field, but a small group of largely educational researchers had begun to question whether these tools alone were the best choice for evaluation.

At this stage of his career, Egon shared his colleagues' optimism in the power of traditional forms of systematic inquiry—the research methodologies of the statistician (experimentation) and the psychometrician (tests and assessments)—to generate useful knowledge for the improvement of educational practice. But there is evidence that by the mid- to late 1960s Egon had begun to question this position.

Dan Stufflebeam (2008, p. 1389) recalls that while Egon was director of the Bureau of Educational Research and Service at Ohio State, "he had a contract to evaluate MPATI (Midwest Program for Airborne Televised Instruction). A DC3 from Purdue University regularly flew around the Midwest during school days while beaming certain courses that a randomly assigned group of selected schools could receive on television sets. Egon's responsibility was to conduct a true experiment through which he would compare student outcomes for schools that got the MPATI courses with a randomly assigned control group of schools that taught the same courses according to past school practices." Although the results of the experiment revealed no statistically significant differences between the experimental and control groups, Egon remained committed to the methodology.

In a subsequent research project funded by Encyclopedia Britannica and Bell and Howell, named Project Discovery, Egon was asked to evaluate the effects on students, teachers, administrators, parents, and the curricula of placing audiovisual equipment and media in four schools in four different regions of the United States. Egon's initial plan to employ a traditional design was thwarted when the funders required that the evaluation be conducted only in the four schools in question without recourse to a design involving experimental and control groups. Instead, the project involved recruiting four resident field observers to each spend approximately nine months at his or her respective site using largely qualitative methods to document the effects of Project Discovery. Stufflebeam (2008) recalls this as perhaps the first excursion into what Egon at the time called 'aexperimental design.'

Shortly after these projects were completed, Egon delivered several papers based on appraisals of what he had learned. The first, in November 1965, was an address to the Conference on Strategies for Educational Change in Washington, DC, entitled "Methodological Strategies for Educational Change." The abstract for that paper read:

> This study of strategies for educational change concludes that the aexperimental, observational, or field study approach is preferred

to the experimental or laboratory approach, both for chan_ search, which is concerned with the entire process of change, and for evaluation, which is concerned with the assessment of single phases of change. Experimental strategy inquires into possibilities, whereas aexperimental strategy inquires into actualities.

Two years later he published a paper entitled "The Expanding Concept of Research" (Guba, 1967) that further revealed how he had begun to question the utility of then dominant means of systematic inquiry for generating knowledge useful for educational change. He argued that "the *concept* [emphasis in original] of what research is and how it may be utilized to affect educational practice is under considerable scrutiny" (p. 57) and that three specific areas of concern were emerging:

> First, it is clear that the traditional techniques of research are not adequate to handle the many questions that can or should be asked about education. Classic models of experimentation, although extremely useful, cannot handle the full range of inquiry. Second, there is a developing interest in establishing better linkages between research and practice....Finally, there is a shift away from questions of mere technique and methodology in research to those concerning the nature of problems, the place of theory, and other aspects of the research activity. (pp. 57–58)

In this paper, Egon, the experimenter, raised a number of critical questions about the utility of experiments for answering the kinds of questions that were most important for effecting educational change. He did not dismiss the study of educational interventions via experimentation as irrelevant but simply pointed out the limitations of that methodology and noted, drawing on the work of the ecological psychologist Roger Barker, that

> there is a second kind of inquiry...in which the investigator does not intervene at all but simply keeps a close record of what occurs. This second mode—which Barker called 'Type T' inquiry and which I call 'aexperimental' inquiry delivers a real-life correspondence not available in the laboratory. On the other hand, the laboratory offers a degree of precision and control that can never be approximated in a field study. (p. 60)

At this point in his career, Egon focused principally on the utility of methodologies for educational research and evaluation. It appears that his interests lay in finding a methodology that would prove useful for promoting educational change in ways that experimentation could not. Egon's concerns were not yet focused on the idea of alternative paradigms, but rather on the value of new ways of studying educational issues and circumstances. As he explained:

> Both forms of inquiry provide valuable information. The experimental approach yields information about a total range of relationships, focuses attention on a highly restricted number of variables as indicated by theory, maintains careful controls, and is highly generalizable because, it is by design, quite context free. The aexperimental approach yields information about relationships as they actually occur in nature, focuses attention on many variables at once, provides a certain flexibility for adjusting to situations that the rigid controls of experimentalism make impossible, and yields a rich and detailed supply of information about a particular happening in a particular context. The laboratory tells what happens in the best of all possible worlds, while the aexperiment tells what happens in the worst. Thus, experimentalism and aexperimentalism are complementary—representing two sides of the same coin. There are times when each is appropriate, depending upon the investigator's intent, the degree of pre-existing knowledge about the phenomenon being studied, and the relative degree of control or flexibility that may be desirable. (Guba, 1967, p. 60)

Concerns about adequate research methodologies were only part of what Guba found relevant to an expanding concept of research. His second concern about research-practice linkages focused on the lack of adequate understanding of what was required to bridge the two. He argued that "the assumption was blithely made that educational research, once published, would by some mysterious process be turned into a practical teaching method or new curriculum" (p. 61) and that what was needed was a focus on the science (even engineering) of 'development' as that was concerned with identifying problems, inventing solutions to those problems, engineering the proposed solutions into practical form, and field testing these packages. He wrote, "Those carrying out these functions may be thought of as educational engineers in a very literal sense. Like the engineers of the hard sciences, they are concerned with utilizing the knowledge produced by the researchers in order to develop practical answers to operating problems" (p. 61).[1]

This concern with development research dovetailed with Egon's growing concerns about the failure of educational evaluation. After hiring Stufflebeam at Ohio State University, Egon became committed to Stufflebeam's conception of evaluation as a decision-support tool for program management, and the two published several papers in the late 1960s on the significance of this approach (Stufflebeam, 2008). But by 1967 a variety of new approaches to evaluation were being introduced by Lee Cronbach, Robert Stake, Elliott Eisner, and others; alternative conceptualizations continued to flourish through the mid- to late 1970s in the work of Malcolm Parlett and David Hamilton, Ernest House, Michael Patton, and Michael Scriven. Egon was aware of and a participant in this community of scholars exploring new ways of conceptualizing evaluation. In a paper delivered in 1969 (Guba, 1969) he argued that there were "clinical signs" of evaluation's failure: that the field was characterized by immobilization rather than responsiveness to evaluation opportunities; that the very agencies that mandated evaluation were unable to provide reasonable and understandable guidelines for doing it; that evaluation consultants consistently provided misadvice to clients who sought their aid in designing or carrying out evaluations; and that evaluations consistently failed to provide useful information. Guba further enumerated a series of 'basic lacks' that he believed contributed to this failure: lack of adequate definition of evaluation; lack of evaluation theory; lack of knowledge about the decision process; lack of criteria on which judgments might be based; lack of approaches

---

1. Egon's third concern in this important paper was the preparation of educational researchers. He was as much interested in the capacity of researchers to adequately conceptualize a research problem, specify research objectives, and articulate a theoretical framework as he was with their methodological preparation. In the mid- to late 1970s, Egon and colleagues (David Clark, Gerald Smith) at Indiana University prepared several internal papers aimed at improving the ability of students in educational doctoral programs to develop research proposals.

differentiated by level of complexity of what was being evaluated; lack of mechanisms for organizing, processing, and reporting evaluative information; and lack of trained personnel.

In the mid-1970s based on his re-appraisal of experiences with contract evaluations at the Ohio State University as well as conversations with colleagues Robert Wolf and others when he moved to Indiana University, Egon began to consider a new approach to evaluation. He delivered a paper in 1977, "Educational Evaluation: The State of the Art," in which he argued that extant models/approaches to evaluation were inadequate and that a science of evaluation must take into account the social and political contexts that surround evaluation.

His thinking about aexperimental methodology and the shortcomings of then current evaluation approaches was brought together in full expression in the 1978 monograph, "Toward a Methodology of Naturalistic Inquiry in Educational Evaluation." This monograph displays the features of naturalistic inquiry as a form of empirical investigation distinct from experimental inquiry but allied with his earlier understanding of aexperimental inquiry. The monograph also briefly explains how naturalistic inquiry is congenial with emerging approaches to evaluation as discussed by Robert Stake, Robert Wolf, Elliot Eisner, Malcom Parlett and David Hamilton, and others; and, it addresses three methodological problems likely faced by those who wish to employ the methodology (boundary problems, focusing problems, and authenticity). Yet, this is still largely a methodological account, dealing, as Egon stated in the introduction to the monograph, with "middle range methodological questions…issues that fall somewhere between the poles of epistemology and technique" (p. 2).

Three years later, with the publication of his book *Effective Evaluation* with co-author Yvonna Lincoln (Guba & Lincoln, 1981), there is a marked deepening and extension of the ideas first presented in the monograph. It is here that the idea of contrasting scientific and naturalistic *paradigms* (not simply experimental and naturalistic methodologies) begins to receive its first expression, with the two paradigms contrasted on their assumptions about (a) reality, (b) the inquirer-subject relationship, and (c) the nature of 'truth' statements. Notions of a constructivist philosophy did not yet formally enter the picture (the term 'constructivism' does not even appear in the index to the book), yet there is brief mention of naturalistic inquirers being concerned with "multiple realities that, like the layers of an onion, nest within or complement one another" (p. 57).

With the publication of *Naturalistic Inquiry* in 1985 (Lincoln & Guba, 1985), the argument about paradigms and their assumptions is further expanded, and, for the first time, a discussion of the idea of "constructed realities" appears. That idea receives even more extensive treatment in *Fourth-Generation Evaluation* published four years later (Guba & Lincoln, 1989) where the notion of a "constructivist paradigm" as a coherent belief system is given full treatment. In *Fourth-Generation Evaluation*, the paradigm in question is no longer called 'naturalistic' but 'constructivist,' and the relativist ontology, subjectivist epistemology, and hermeneutic methodology of constructivism are even more sharply contrasted with the realist ontology, objectivist epistemology, and interventionist methodology of the 'conventional' belief system. By no means were matters of methodology or method neglected in these developing accounts of a constructivist paradigm for evaluation. The 1978 monograph and the subsequent three books all contained extensive discussions of what doing naturalistic (and later, constructivist) inquiry in practice entailed. Yet, it is clear that in the successive iterations of his ideas, Egon's work is ever more focused specifically on the idea of competing paradigms for inquiry that rest on fundamentally different belief systems. Articulating the content and structure of the belief system of a constructivist paradigm becomes the primary object of interest and analysis, culminating in what he and Lincoln now offer as *The Constructivist Credo*.

References

Clark, D. L., & Guba, E. G. (1965, October). "An Examination of Potential Change Roles in Education." Paper presented at the Seminar on Innovation in Planning School Change, Columbus, Ohio.

Clark, D. L., & Guba, E. G. (1972). A re-examination of a test of the 'Research and Development Model' of change, *Educational Administration Quarterly*, 8(3), 93–103.

Guba, E. G. (1965). "Methodological Strategies for Educational Change." Paper presented to the Conference on Strategies for Educational Change, sponsored by the Ohio State University and the U.S. Office of Education, in Washington, DC.

Guba, E. G. (1967). The expanding concept of research. *Theory Into Practice, 6*(2), 57–65.

Guba, E. G. (1969). The failure of educational evaluation. *Educational Technology, 9,* 29–38.

Guba, E. G. (1978). "Toward a Methodology of Naturalistic Inquiry in Educational Evaluation." CSE Monograph No. 8. UCLA Center for the Study of Evaluation. Los Angeles: Center for the Study of Evaluation.

Guba, E. G., & Clark, D. L. (1975). The configurational perspective: A new view of educational knowledge production and utilization. *Educational Researcher, 4*(4), 6–9.

Guba, E. G., & Lincoln, Y. S. (1981). *Effective evaluation.* San Francisco: Jossey-Bass.

Guba, E. G., & Lincoln, Y. S. (1989). *Fourth-generation evaluation.* Beverly Hills, CA: Sage.

Kerr, C. (1963). *The uses of the university.* Cambridge, MA: Harvard University Press.

Lincoln, Y. S., & Guba, E. G. (1985). *Naturalistic inquiry.* Beverly Hills, CA: Sage.

Stufflebeam, D. L. (2008). Egon Guba's conceptual journey to constructivist evaluation. *Qualitative Inquiry, 14*(8), 1386–1400.

Thomas. J. (1975). Political science and education: Points of contact. In S. Nagel (Ed.), *Policy studies and the social sciences* (pp. 135–148). New Brunswick, NJ: Transaction.

The Constructivist Credo

Yvonna S. Lincoln
Egon G. Guba

My Aim and Hope

Egon G. Guba

Stephen Jay Gould, in *Eight Little Piggies* (1993), comments on the work of Johann Wolfgang Goethe, the celebrated German poet, who, as an avocation, devoted considerable effort to the study of morphology:

> Goethe published his most important biological work in 1790—*Versuch die Metamorphose der Pflanzen zu erk/aren* (An attempt to explain the metamorphosis of plants). This work, a pamphlet devoid of illustrations or charts and consisting of 125 numbered, largely aphoristic, passages can scarcely be called a document of conventional science. It embodies the two principles that Goethe attributed to his artistic predilections—bold hypotheses based on assumptions of inherent unity. And yet, though Goethe's central notion cannot be sustained, this curious little work is full of insight and has exerted a strong influence over the history of morphology (a word coined by Goethe). (p. 158)

I can scarcely claim to be a poet, not to mention one of Goethe's stature. I have nevertheless attempted to emulate Goethe: By working from an assumption of inherent unity (although I would prefer to term it inherent integrity), to suggest that what contructivism and

The Constructivist Credo, by Yvonna S. Lincoln and Egon G. Guba. 27–31

constructivist inquiry are, and what constructivist inquirers should do, *may be derived*—at least in the form of reasonable conjectures—from a small number of metaphysical presumptions, ontological, epistemological, axiological and methodological in nature, which I have [arbitrarily?] taken as axiomatic (but not in the sense of self-evident).

While it is unexceptional, this approach unfortunately begs the question of what logical rules shall be followed in making that derivation. The phrase, if derived as I have used it above, is misleading, for it suggests, at least in ordinary discourse, that constructivist characteristics and actions can logically be deduced from the underlying metaphysical presuppositions in the same way that, for example, the theorems of Euclidean geometry can be deduced ("proved") from Euclid's four axioms. That conclusion would be warranted if and only if the rules applied in the derivation were those of classical logic. But those rules, it has become increasingly apparent, are unnecessarily constraining; other "logics" exist, analogous to the way in which multiple sets of defining presumptions exist.

Most questionable of these rules is the well-known "Law of the Excluded Middle." That law conveniently divides all propositions into two classes: true and false. The human mind finds such dualisms congenial; dualisms are rampant in the history of Western thought: Soma/pysche, body/soul, good/evil, energy/matter, monism/pluralism, liberal/conservative, self/other, part/whole, animate/ inanimate, concrete/abstract, rational/emotional, sacred/profane, and the like. This true/false dualism leads to the conclusion that any proposition that is not true must be false. If, however, we permit the excluded middle to take on several possible values ("sometimes true," "true only if...," "true only until midnight of December 31, 2015, but false thereafter..."), wholly different logics might emerge. The common dualism true/false dissolves into a continuum. Linearity becomes chaos. Reductionism becomes multiplism. Impeccable logic becomes fuzzy logic. We thus come face to face with a mind-boggling dilemma. Any particular paradigm may be constructed by intersecting two dimensions: one defining the particular ontological, epistemological, axiological and methodological presumptions (metaphysics) on which we propose to proceed, and the other defining the particular logic to be utilized in deriving the consequences of those presumptions. From a theoretical point of view, the number of different possible paradigms generated from such intersections is as limitless as the number of different metaphysical presumptions and different logics, and all their combinations, that can be imagined. From a practical point of view, their number is probably much more delimited but nevertheless quite large, probably too large to be individually pursued, given present levels of information and sophistication.

What I propose to do in this brief treatise, then, is necessarily as much intuitive—an educated guess—as it is logical. I choose a particular metaphysics which I believe provides the most informed and sophisticated fit for social inquiry, but I follow loose, informal rules of logic rather than well-defined, formal ones. My passages, akin to Goethe's, will be "largely aphoristic," more conjectural than definitive. As implications of a constructivist metaphysics, these passages are incomplete, and many may be undecidable. The set would clearly not be dubbed a "document of conventional science." It may nevertheless stimulate thought and discussion, leading to assessment and reformulation.

Let me return for a moment to the notion that Goethe in some sense sets the pattern for the passages that follow. I shall early on make the point that conceptual sense-making—what I call *developing a construction*—consists of the semiotic organization of terms and their interrelationships in ways that allow the constructor both to crystallize them in his or her own mind as well as to communicate them to others. Traditionally, science has sought to devise terms that correspond to (are isomorphic with) the presumptively *real* entities for which they stand. I prefer, as a constructivist, to think of a construction as little more than a metaphor, not for something "real," but as a way of making sense of something.

It is in this sense that what I do here may be thought of as poetic, because most of the passages that I set out strike me as metaphors for something that's in my head but which I cannot express with precision. I sometimes think that this effort to set out a series of conjectures is nothing more than an effort to educate myself, to try to make clearer and more tangible what I "know" only at a tacit level, or incompletely. But there is a further complication. Since what I "know" is itself a construction, it is subject to continuous change—to reconstruction—as available information and sophistication improve. My effort to focus more clearly on my tacit constructions is thus confounded by the fact that I am aiming at a moving target. That insight clarifies for me why it is that successive formulations of a construction cannot be "more true" than their precursors, but only more informed and sophisticated.

Years ago I read a book, whose author and title I have long forgotten [PACE, forgotten one!], that dealt with the question, "Can one think without using language to do it?" The book consisted of a series of case studies intended to demonstrate that "language-less" thought was possible. I was especially struck by the case of a British mathematician, who claimed that he thought not only without language but without the notational systems common to mathematicians. Indeed, he argued, he developed his proofs at some inner level of mind that eschewed both words and symbols. But when the proof had to be written down so that it could be communicated to others, it "lost in the translation"; that is, it communicated only the surface of the thought and failed to communicate the deeper mental experience. There was much that remained behind, and it was that residue that subsumed much of the "beauty" and "elegance" of the formulation, and perhaps something of its meaning.

I suppose we've all had the experience of working very hard to explain something to someone but coming away with the feeling that we had not communicated all that we might have. There is that residue problem again; no matter how careful and thorough we are in our explanation, we cannot seem to get across everything that we might have wanted, that we associated with the concept. I feel that way about the following passages as well. They represent the best I can do now to communicate my thoughts—my construction—about what constructivism is and what actions are required of us if we claim allegiance to it. If my best is still not very good, well, perhaps that is a matter of unclear or "wrong" logic, to which I have already admitted. Perhaps it is a matter of the moving target; my construction changes faster than I can define it. Perhaps it is a matter of my construction being at least partly tacit. So I fall back on something like poetry or metaphor. What I record here is suggestive of my construction without communicating it either well or completely. My ambition, as I consider my failings, is only to be able to write about constructivism in ways that fit Alexander Pope's advice in his *Essay on Criticism*:

True wit is Nature to advantage dress'd,
What oft was thought, but ne'er so well expressed.

We cannot warrant, although we may hope, that others will find these conjectures bold, curious, and full of insight, and that on some they will exert a strong influence, even if, in the end, they should prove to be "not sustainable." We would find our work meaningful if that turned out to be the case.

This effort to capture the basic presuppositions and their implications for human inquiry is a work in progress, probably very far from completion. The version recorded here is the fifteenth iteration, and may have been further developed by the time it comes into the hands of any reader. I would welcome reactions from anyone: Questions, additions, deletions, challenges, and other emendations. You need have no fear that they will arrive too late; I expect to be at this task for a very long time.

A final word: Perhaps some of my readers will recognize in these pages thoughts, distinctions, and arguments that they have themselves recorded in the literature, without what they might believe to be sufficient attribution. I find it difficult after years of thinking about constructivism to continue to separate the contributions of others from my own. My dear late friend Edgar Dale was wont to comment how surprised he was from time to time to discover how much Shakespeare had plagiarized his writing! In that spirit I beg forgiveness for any authorial oversights. That must especially be the case with the contributions I have gleaned from conversations and discussions with students and my long-time collaborator and spouse, Yvonna S. Lincoln, to whom I remain indebted beyond measure.

EGG
College Station, Texas
July 10, 1995–2006

What This Book Is Not

Readers should understand that neither of us is or was unmindful of the enormously important epistemological, theoretical or methodological debates that swirled around the deployment of alternative paradigm inquiry and qualitative methods. Quite the opposite. Norman Denzin and I, Yvonna, had begun the *SAGE Handbook of Qualitative Research* series, prompted by Mitch Allen, who was at the time a senior editor at Sage, and we had also embarked on the journal co-editorship for *Qualitative Inquiry* at Mitch's encouragement. Egon read chapters in the handbooks, articles in the journal, and many other books, as did I, and we talked endlessly about the multiple meanings of various revolutions in thinking for constructivist inquirers: postmodernism, poststructuralism, "language games," critical theoretical formulations, the impetus toward participatory research and participatory action research (highly influential in our thinking). And we struggled with the "theoretical navigations" provided by the lenses and perspectives rapidly being developed: feminist theories, postcolonial theories, race and ethnic theoretical standpoints, poststructuralism, postmodernism, Deleuzian critiques, Foucauldian archaeologies, border and hybridity theories, Latino critical theories ("LatCrit"), queer theory, and a virtual feast

The Constructivist Credo, by Yvonna S. Lincoln and Egon G. Guba. 33–35

of other theoretical and quasi-theoretical perspectives that began to shape and inform qualitative and alternative paradigm research.

We were not immune to the compelling arguments provided especially by postmodernism—that there is no singular truth; that no method provides such elusive truth; that all methods which claim to produce "truth" or "the real world" fall under immediate suspicion of arrogant overreaching; that there is no final "reading" of any text, but rather that texts invite multiple readings depending on the reader(s) of it, the readers' context and standpoint, and the purposes for which the text is to be read. A deep flavor of that postmodern influence will be seen in the lines—and between the lines—of this text as well. In the insistence on multiple voices, readers will see likewise a tilt toward assuring that women's voices and the voices of those traditionally marginalized will be heard, and re-presented in any texts produced as a part of an inquiry. In the press toward action and tactical help in producing positive and socially just action embedded in the quality criteria, the reader will see the influence of both the critical qualitative researchers' work (particularly that of Kincheloe and McLaren and also of Cannella) and the participatory action researchers' work (particularly the statements of Kemmis and McTaggart in the first and second editions of the *Handbook of Qualitative Research,* as well as those of Greenwood and Levin in the same editions). Indeed, we were—and I continue to be—influenced heavily by the deep theoretical architectures and structures being created and unearthed, and the profoundly methodical, archaeological critiques of methodological migrations that form the interior examinations of a maturing field.

What did not strike us at the time we began this work (although it spanned nearly twelve years, off and on, of conversation, deliberation and setting ideas on paper) were the influences of the critique of neoliberalism, and its corporatist, globalizing, capitalistic pressures on the research university. It wasn't until after Egon's death that I began to read heavily in those critiques as well as confronting them in my own professional life. Since undertaking to complete this work, I have seen firsthand the tyranny of accountability, the managerial focus on the assessment of minutiae and measurable outcomes (ignoring the unmeasurable and far more important work of a university), the despotic and ruthless emphasis on external funding (in the wake of declining state expenditures on higher education, as well as on public education), the glowering disinterest in genuinely creative thought in the aftermath of the "counting culture" surrounding promotion and tenure, the shrinking frames of academic freedom as parttime, adjunct, and contingent faculty replace tenure-bearing lines, and the mistrustful, panopticonic surveillance of faculty worklife as the cult of efficiency and profit overtake the production of knowledge and education for responsible citizenship.

Those issues, however, do not constitute the core of this work. Our purpose was far more modest and limited. What we sought to engage were the deep assumptions, perspectives and presumptions that one might make or adopt were one to engage constructivist inquiry. It is, if you will, a kind of roadmap to the decision structures, the concerns and issues, the nature of the suppositions with which a researcher might be confronted in the field and in the preparation and authorship or co-authorship (with stakeholders) of any text. As we pointed out earlier, many of these assumptions and presumptions arose from questions faced by us or by our students. In the struggle for answers to our and their problems, the nature of the "givens" in constructivist inquiry became clearer.

Thus, we have not taken up the serious debates among theories, lenses, perspectives, and critiques pursued by our colleagues, but rather have focused on extending and clarifying the perspectives of constructivists (and, in Appendix A, tried to imagine what a Tier 1 research university would look like if organized around constructivist principles, rather than scientific method principles). In the process, we have repeated some of our earlier work, although our mission here was to systematize a somewhat longer and more extensive (and scattered) body of work spanning more than twenty years. We hope that we have succeeded in seducing our readers into the text sufficiently to understand that the choice of a paradigm represents a far-ranging and comprehensive professional commitment, influencing professional choices over a lifetime.

Part 1

The Presumptions

Throughout history philosophers concerned with the nature of knowledge and inquiry have posed four fundamental questions:

1. The *ontological* question: "What is there that can be known?" Or, to rephrase the question, "What is the nature of reality?"

2. The *epistemological* question: "What is the nature of the relationship between the knower and the knowable?" The answer one can give to this question is constrained by the answer previously given to the ontological question.

3. The *methodological* question: "How does one go about acquiring knowledge?" The answer one can give to this question is in turn constrained by the answers previously given to the ontological and epistemological questions.

4. The *axiological* question: Of all the knowledge available to me, which is the most valuable, which is the most truthful, which is the most beautiful, which is the most life-enhancing?

The Constructivist Credo, by Yvonna S. Lincoln and Egon G. Guba. 37–41
© 2013 Left Coast Press, Inc. All rights reserved.

There are many ways in which these questions can be answered. Traditionally, reality has been believed to be concrete and tangible, "out there," ultimately determinable by inquiry carried out in a thorough and determined way. That has been until recently the conventional position taken by most scientists. And if reality is so defined, it follows that inquiry about it must be objectively carried out to discover "how things *really* are and *really* work." That requirement in turn suggests a methodology which is essentially experimental and manipulative, in an effort to sort out the various influences ("variables") that determine the true state of affairs, and eliminate the confounding ones.

But there are other positions that can be taken. Recently philosophers of science have argued that while an ultimate reality exists, it cannot be determined with finality (because of the Heisenberg Uncertainty Principle, among other things). Furthermore, the drive toward objectivity has been stunted or thwarted by the realization that scientific work, being conducted by humans who can never escape their emotions and values, can never be authentically objective. Given that state of affairs, the scientific strategy has therefore become one of *managing subjectivity* as tenaciously as possible, to come as near to "truth" as human frailty permits. Experimentation and manipulation are retained as the basic methodological strategy, even while it is conceded that they cannot produce ultimately infallible results.

It might be acceptable to conclude that in the physical and biological sciences, such an approach is reasonably appropriate (although that conclusion is by no means secure). But suppose one decides to define reality in a non-foundational sense, that is, relativistically. What if reality is conceptualized as not being real in the usual sense, but relative to its observer/definer? Is there a class of entities worth inquiring into that would fit this definition? We believe it to be the case that all entities commonly included within the purview of the human sciences are of this kind. We would argue that every social/psychological/cultural entity with which practitioners of the human sciences deal exists only in this non-concrete, intangible form. For example, the meaning of entities such as "school," "personality," "values," intelligence," "morality," "leadership," "poverty," "democracy," "gender," "race," and the myriad other "variables" in whose terms human scientists are accustomed to think and to theorize depends entirely on the definer (despite efforts to concretize such variables via "operational" definitions). Thus, relativism is the key.

The purpose of this treatise is to propose a systematic way—which we call constructivism—of answering the four basic questions that start with the presupposition that social reality is relative to the individuals involved and to the particular context in which they find themselves. Change the individuals and you change the reality. Or change the context and you change the reality. Or change both the individuals and the context and thoroughly change the reality. And if you make that ontological redefinition, obviously you greatly alter the presuppositions it is reasonable to make at the epistemological and methodological, as well as the axiological, levels.

The answers, provided by constructivism for the four paradigm-defining questions, follow. Proposed answers to these questions cannot be tested in any foundational way; they can be accepted or rejected only by virtue of their pragmatic utility. It is by extension and extrapolation from these presuppositions that the conjectures of Part 2 arise.

CAVEAT: Recall that both presumptions and conjectures are intended to apply only to the human sciences! We would still contend that in the physical sciences, quite possibly the experimental "scientific method" may be the most useful tool for exploring the physical and natural world.

Ontology
Relativism is the basic ontological presupposition of constructivism.

In the human sciences, entities are matters of definition and convention; they exist only in the minds of the persons contemplating them. They do not "really" exist. That is, they have ontological status only insofar as some group of persons (frequently, social scientists, but often the rest of us, also) grants them that status.

Epistemology
Transactional subjectivism is the basic presupposition of constructivism.

Given that the ontological presupposition of relativism has been accepted, it follows that the relationship between the knower and the knowable (to-be-known) is highly person- and context-specific. The "realities" taken to exist depend on a transaction between the knower and the "to-be-known" in the particular context in which the encounter between them takes place. That transaction is necessarily highly subjective, mediated by the knower's prior experience and knowledge, by political and social status, by gender, by race, class, sexual orientation, nationality, by personal and cultural values, and by the knower's interpretation (construction) of the contextual surround. Knowledge is not "discovered" but rather _created_; it exists only in the time/space framework in which it is generated.

Methodology
Hermeneutic/dialecticism is the basic methodological presupposition of constructivism.

Given that the ontological presupposition of relativism and the epistemological presupposition of transactional subjectivism have been accepted, it follows that the methodology appropriate to constructivism must be one that delves into the minds and meaning-making, sense-making activities of the several knowers involved. Two processes are required. First, it is essential to uncover the constructions held by the various knowers; this is best accomplished by a process whereby the constructions are successively disclosed and plumbed for meaning. The meanings are best found by having research participants work together with inquirers as equals, sharing the nomination of issues deemed critical to both parties, and pursuing those topics together. The well-known interpretive/explanatory method of hermeneutics seems most appropriate. Second, the various constructions held by individual knowers must be confronted, compared, and contrasted in an encounter situation; the well-known dialogue/argumentation method of dialectics seems most appropriate.

Axiology

Values inhere in every human project;
objectivity is a chimera.

Rather than assuming that scientific projects can be brought closer and closer to objectivity, objectivity—at least as it is conjured by the strict positivists and those who claim the right to define "science" (National Research Council, 2002)—is rejected as a possibility when inquirer and research participants act together to co-create knowledge and create a new, shared reality. In this shared and co-created reality, the values of the inquirer, the various value systems of research participants, the values which inhere in the context all must be uncovered and made transparent. It is also the case that, ultimately, the values of stakeholders in the research—those who are not participants but for whom the research itself is important, or informs some part of their work or their lives—will come into play.

The conjectures that follow are, we believe, consequences (broadly defined) of these four presumptive definitions, although it remains to be seen whether they will be found worthy on close scrutiny and by attempts to apply them.

Part 2

The Conjectures

In the following pages, we lay out 130 or so conjectures. These 130 plus conjectures are themselves (we believe) derivative from the metaphysics of constructivism—the ontology, epistemology, axiology, and methodology discussed earlier. But they have been suggested to us either via our own research and evaluation activities, or by our students, who encountered conundra as a part of their own deep explorations into research (primarily their dissertation research, but occasionally, work they undertook after taking their first professorial position). Our attempt here is merely to lay them out as we believe we "found" them— sorted and categorized, of course, for some kind of easy reference—for the purposes of contemplation. It's our hope that readers will find resonance and some coalescence with their own field experiences, writing adventures, or reflexive journaling.

The Constructivist Credo, by Yvonna S. Lincoln and Egon G. Guba. 43–82
© 2013 Left Coast Press, Inc. All rights reserved.

Basic Definitions

Presumption: An assumption that is taken for granted in some piece of reasoning; belief on reasonable evidence.

Implication: The relation that holds between two propositions or classes of propositions by virtue of which one is logically deducible from the other.

Conjecture: A conclusion or supposition from inadequate or insufficient grounds to ensure proof, inviting further investigation.

Human inquiry: Research, evaluation, and policy analysis carried out in relation to human beings.

A—In the Beginning

A1. Human beings experience an inchoate world, a buzzing, bumbling confusion, a confounded surround, that challenges their very survival. As Elliot Eisner has suggested (1993 AERA presidential address), "This world is immediate before it is mediated, presentational before it is representational, sensuous before it is symbolic." Or, as Reason has put it (1994), "In original participation human beings are embedded in their world, consciousness is undifferentiated, there is no separation between subject and object, and little reflectiveness" (p. 22).

A2. There is no compelling reason to believe, a priori, that this surround has any existence apart from the individuals who encounter it, that is, to believe it to be objectively independent of the sense mechanisms of the individuals who experience it.

A3. Encounters within the surround—with objects, events, and life forms including other persons—provide a store of sensory memories which the individual processes into forms that seem to "make sense," that is, forms that organize—reconstruct—sense experiences and make them meaningful. This world is made sensible—that is, made to make sense—by the order that human beings impose on events, situations and circumstances.

A4.   Sense-making is an effort by human beings, utilizing the constructive character of the mind and limited only by the imagination, to deal with confusion by means of a semiotic organization—an assemblage of signs and symbols, not only verbal but including many different forms of representation—that attaches meanings to "realized" elements [elements made real?] selectively abstracted from the otherwise confounded surround.

A5.   Sense-specific ways of expressing this idea may include such as, for example, "getting the feel of things," "hearing the bell ring," "smelling it out," "getting in touch," or "seeing it." Elliot Eisner (1993) uses the phrase "getting in touch," which he defines as "an act of discrimination, a fine-grained sensitively nuanced process in which the mind is fully engaged."

A6.   Sense-making is an act of construal. Humans do not merely experience events, they create them. Construal, not discovery, is the critical act of perception and construction.

A7.   Making sense of something means organizing it and rendering it into apparently comprehensible, understandable, and explainable form (giving it form and substance) so that it is possible to cope with it, turning it from a random congeries of sense impressions into something that can be ordered and fitted into a larger conceptual structure, theory, discipline, or philosophy (most of which will nevertheless have only local, or perhaps even only personal, significance).

A8.   Sense-making need not be conscious, or limited to cognitive or logical sense-making; it is likely that many sense-making activities are tacit (not available for expression in language form) rather than propositional (able to be stated in formal language). Propositional sense-makings thus necessarily focus on limited and frequently shared aspects of human experience, simultaneously limiting human ability to articulate and to share experiences. That fact does not, however, constrain or eliminate tacit sense-making per se. It only suggests that making sense of one's surround occurs in two forms: the tacit, or unspoken (and perhaps unspeakable, as, for instance, when we speak of "women's intuition" or "gut-level hunches"), and the propositional, that which is able to be formally rendered into language and symbols.

In many instances, engaging in qualitative and constructivist work involves the difficult task of attempting to "bring forth" the tacit by struggling to render such knowledge or understandings into words. Some authors speak of "wrapping words" around a tacit construction, and this is likely a poetic, but perfectly accurate, way of describing the struggle.

A9. Sense-making does not often take the form of clean, logical distinctions. The sense characterizations made of experienced phenomena are often "fuzzy" in nature, as that term is used to describe "fuzzy logic" (Kosko, 1993). As Kosko puts it, fuzzy systems are "grown" from data. In much the same manner, constructions and co-constructions are "grown," or created, from the data generated between researcher and participants. That is, new constructions "boil down the clustering data into rules" (Kosko, 1993, p. 221).

A10. Sense making, or the creation of constructions, is independent of any social foundational reality (if such in fact exists); it does not result in objective truth, but only in sets of symbols and meanings defined and applied by humans to enhance their ability to deal with the surround, to survive, cope, and prosper.

We do mean to clarify here that we are engaging the social world, rather than the natural world. When we talk about sense-making, we are largely, if not solely, dealing with the world created by and for humans interacting with other humans and other beings.

A11. Thus, "reality," "truth" (including truth viewed as a "regulatory ideal"), and "fact" are all relative concepts—they are themselves semiotic signs that are relative to the person(s) who hold particular sense-makings, constructions, or meanings. An excellent example of this is the 2002 National Research Council report, *Scientific Research in Education,* which attempts to lay down the rules of what constitutes science—and what does not. In the construction of the National Research Council, qualitative research may be "scholarship" but it is "not science." As Hannah Arendt so succinctly put it, "Truth is coercive." [1]

CAVEAT: That assertion does not imply that "anything goes." Qualitative researchers, particularly social constructivists, have been accused of a certain Feyerabendian bent toward believing that anything goes. Nothing could be farther from the truth. In a later section in this work, we talk about standards for quality work, including attending to the community standards that support social justice, egalitarianism, equity of opportunity, and other liberal values.

B—Constructions

B1.   A construct is a mental realization—"a making real"—of an apparently singular, unitary entity or relationship; an element of a construction.

B2.   A construction is a coherent, articulated set of constructs—a pattern or web of constructs and their interconnections—that makes sense of some aspect (some "chunk") of the constructor's surround. It need not be verbal but can take many different representational forms.

B3.   Constructions are the end products of individual (and sometimes group) efforts at sense-making, and hence they are inherently subjective. This does not mean that they can never be shared. Many aspects of constructions are frequently shared between individuals who hold similar values or beliefs, or who, for a variety of reasons (think again of class, race, gender, sexual orientation, political leanings, religious upbringing, and the like), "see" the world in the same way.

---

1.   This quotation is widely attributed to Hannah Arendt, but I cannot find this set of words in anything published. It is quite likely that this particular framing was used in an oral delivery of her paper "Truth and Politics," cited herein. In the published version, the quotation is "Truth has in it an inherent coercion" (2008, p. 298).

B4.   The scope of constructions (especially their form) is limited, for a given constructor, by the forms of representation (verbal, emotional, artistic, performative, and others) which he or she has previously learned and with which he or she feels comfortable.

B5.   Different representations of constructions lead to different outcomes or products, different ways of expressing experience.

B6.   An important feature of constructions is that they can be manipulated and modified (by interrelating, interpolating, extrapolating, or metaphoric leap) into new and unexpected configurations, resulting in possibilities not directly encountered in experience; they can give rise to creative and innovative formulations that extend human thought and appreciation, or, additionally, extend social justice.

   In fact, this is what most of education is about: the creation of critical capabilities, and the rich extension of interiority, emotional intelligence, and creative and compassionate capacity.

B7.   Any given construction is characterized by some level of meanings (the substance or content of the construction) and some level of sophistication in the use of those meanings (organizing, formatting, interpreting, and interrelating them).

B8.   Constructions may be simple or complex, lower-level or higher-level, small-scale or large-scale, ranging from simple naming of entities to complex theories and paradigms, music, performances, artifacts, other material expressions, and the like.

B9.   Constructions need not be developed de novo by every individual; they may be developed jointly with other individuals or learned from them (indeed, education may be characterized as the acquisition of existing constructions by means of a formal process). Culture itself is also a powerful transmitter of constructions, and some of the constructions we carry around with us are "inherited" from our culture, our social standing, or our "standpoints," that is, our race, class, gender, religious upbringing, socio-economic status, political preferences, the geographic region in which we grew up, nationality, sexual orientation, and a virtually endless array of social, cultural, educational, and military experiences.

B10. Constructions, whether formed de novo, individually, developed jointly, learned, or absorbed culturally, are open to continuous reconstruction, as reflection on new or accumulated experience or on inputs and challenges from other individuals leads to new or added meanings and/or sophistication (advanced education may be characterized as learning how to develop and/or extend existing constructions and/or to develop new ones, as well as learning how to engage in critical reflexivity in order to test one's constructions on a periodic basis).

B11. Personal as well as cultural identities are formed and understood through interactions between and among multiple individuals situated in the same, or metaphorically or vicariously similar, surround.

It is also the case, however, that personal and/or cultural identities may be formed and understood through interactions between and among multiple individuals and groups situated in *radically different surrounds*, as, for instance, when individuals travel to culturally strange, exotic and different places and are exposed to extremely different lifeways and cultural patterns, and must cope with what amounts to counter-cultural reprogramming. This is one reason college students who live abroad for some extended period of time frequently return more mature, more tolerant, more deeply empathic than they were prior to the experience. As their interactions between and among individuals and groups who live very differently are expanded and the new culture understood and accepted on its own terms, individuals form broader capacities for understanding, and consequently, identities which are able to consider and reflect upon constructions not previously entertained.

B12. Individuals experience a press for fit and harmony within and between constructions which they hold; the attainment (or near attainment) of such harmony is an essential condition for stability of personality (itself a construction).

Maturity, however, extends the ability of the individual to consider and, frequently, nonjudgmentally reflect upon constructions which others may hold, and which are at variance with his or her own. The ability to listen actively and deeply (a requisite for sound constructivist/interpretivist inquiry) depends on this ability to hear and entertain constructions different from one's own beliefs, attitudes, and values.

B13.   Similarly, individuals who are situated in a common physical or intellectual surround experience a press for fit and harmony among the constructions held by them severally; the attainment (or near attainment) of such harmony is the essential condition for stability of their common culture (also a construction).

   While this conjecture may appear abstract, it nevertheless has very practical implications. For instance, the so-called "paradigm wars" (of which this book is a piece of the argument; see, for instance, Gage, 1989) are a strong example of what happens when paradigmatic controversy enters the academy. Some faculty and students, sensing the "fit" of a new paradigm with the questions they ask and the inquiries they propose, become early adopters. Other faculty, seeking to defend what they do, stoutly resist any and all efforts to admit such inquiries to the body of knowledge, even seeking to define such inquiries as "not science." Knorr-Cetina and Mulkay (1983) label this second set of inquirers the "priesthood" who defend "sacerdotal science" as the only true "religion" of the scientific community, indicating the stance many have taken as defenders of the practices and methods with which they are most familiar.

B14.   Personal or cultural disharmony, including social injustice, may be the necessary springboard for the need for therapy, for political action, and/or for the need for inquiry.

   Indeed, one controversy which is currently being engaged is the extent to which inquiry can or cannot be utilized for advocacy purposes, that is, whether or not science can be linked to political action (particularly on behalf of redressing social injustice, or making transparent the structures and hidden infrastructures that reify social inequality).

B15.   Constructions are conditioned upon and impacted by ontological, epistemological, axiological, teleological, and methodological presumptions and the social, cultural, historical, political, economic, ethnic, and gender values (touchstones invoked at choice points) held by the individuals who devise them. Those presumptions and values are themselves constructions.

B16. While constructions make possible the synthesis of personal experience and the communication of that experience to others, they also miscommunicate by virtue of unavoidable inclusion/exclusion decisions, abstractions, shapings, and other simplifications and abbreviations, and including especially neglected or unnoticed tacit constructions (especially those surrounding *race, class, gender, and sexual orientation*), biases or prejudices.

B17. Since constructions are the products of individual or shared sense-making efforts in an otherwise inchoate world, they cannot represent foundational realities or truths; they are literally the creation of the interaction between and among individuals and their surround. This is another way of saying that the categories we choose for sense-making purposes are not "givens" from the cosmos. We *create* those categories—for example, race, gender, social class, nationality—in order to engage in that very sensemaking.

B18. Truth is a quality of a construct or construction; constructs or constructions are "true" to the extent that they enable the constructor better to cope with (comprehend, understand, explain, order, fit, make sense of) the realized or constituent element(s).

B19. The credibility, believability, or "truth value" of any assertions about "reality" and "truth" depends solely on the meaning sets (information) available to the audiences for the assertion(s).

Audiences, stakeholders and/or inquirers may have access to sound information, or may have access only to misinformation or disinformation. It is also the case that audiences may have access to sound, that is, factual, information, but choose to ignore such information in favor of their own biased or prejudicial information. A stark example is useful here: In the recent presidential campaign, one candidate remarked to a high-income audience ($50,000 per plate) that "47 percent of Americans pay no taxes" and are therefore "takers" rather than contributors to the common purse. The candidate's statement misleads the audience by failing to note that the 47 percent are comprised of those whose incomes fall so far below the poverty line that they owe no taxes; that a significant number of those citizens are unemployed and consequently have no income on which to pay taxes; are disabled, cannot work, and are receiving legitimate disability payments; or are retired and earning no income save for Social Security, for which they have contributed over a lifetime of earnings. The disinformation indicated by this statement suited the audience well; it was what they wanted to hear. But the statement misled, and thus deliberately provided no truth value for the audience to consider.

C—Shared Constructions

C1. Constructions may be shared among individuals, that is, the assemblage of signs and symbols (the semiotic organization) and of meanings of which that assemblage is comprised may be held in common by two or more individuals.

C2. Holding a construction does not mean that one has the ability to share it; not all constructors can be articulate about their constructions, just as not all connoisseurs can be critics. To say this another way, some constructions may be tacit. In that instance, the holder of the construction may not even be aware of the construction.

C3. The "regularities" of human behavior often observed by social scientists, many of which they have tended to label as generalizations, are evidence of nothing more than shared constructions. Patterns and regularities seem to occur because the individuals studied share constructions, not because those constructions reflect some "natural" event or law.

   This is especially true if the individuals studied have all been men, as Ruth Bleier (1988) and Marion Namenwirth (1988) point out. Generalizations about "mankind" tend to revolve about either the concerns of the white, male, middle-class researchers conducting the inquiry, or the white, male, middle-class individuals who populate the sample studied. They rarely speak any "truth" about women's concerns, women's issues, or the viewpoints of women. Consider, for example, the question of whether a low-dose aspirin a day is the right prescription for women to guard against strokes or heart attacks. Since all the studies conducted to date have involved such prescriptions for men, and since women "present" differently for strokes and heart attacks, what might be the right preventive treatment for women? Studies are currently underway, but we have no definitive scientific evidence about what might work for women.

C4. Attempts to apply such putative generalizations in particular local contexts produces a "social Heisenberg effect," making the impact of the application locally indeterminate. The application disturbs the context and guarantees non-conformity to the generalization (a prime reason why "theory into practice" so often fails).

C5. Sharing may occur as the result of joint development of constructions, by learning, or by socialization. Joint development is one of the "strong" arguments for collaborative research among inquirers, and learning and socializations one of the "strong" arguments for involving graduate students in research projects.

C6. Shared constructions require shared experiences, and shared experiences require shared constructions; efforts at common sense-making require some base of prior experience/construction commonality.

C7. Experience can be shared vicariously, as for example, by word of mouth, via a journal article, or through a case study. Vicarious sharing is the chief means of applying experience gained by persons in one setting by receivers in other settings, by suggesting, directly or metaphorically, ways in which the receivers' existing construction(s) might be modified, adapted, or challenged.

C8. A shared construction need not be formed or held in identical ways by individuals sharing it; a common consensual core may be surrounded by more peripheral elements which differ in greater or lesser degree from person to person. This is especially the case with tacit elements of constructions.

C9. Shared constructions need not be (and often are not) shared by all parties affected by them (the stakeholders). The question of whose voice is heard in any given construction is thus as much an ethical *and political* as a factual one.

C10. Shared constructions, especially among larger groups of individuals, become reified over time to become part of the sociocultural milieu. They may be jointly reviewed, edited, and stabilized; physical, historical, social, and cultural "realities" are thereby rendered tangible and concrete (and most importantly, come to be seen as unchangeable; compare "divided consciousness" and "false consciousness"). Nevertheless, constructions, even when shared as a part of the sociocultural milieu, are not reality but continue to be mental assemblages of semiotic signs and symbols, of meanings and meaning sets. They become what critical theorists term "historically reified" or "historical reality."

C11. Shared constructions may exhibit several levels of putative generality. Individual "objects" may be collected into several generic classes, which may in turn be collected into several theories, which, when taken together, form the several "knowledges" (as that term is commonly used; constructivists might prefer the phrase, different "meaning sets") extant in a given culture. A good example would be "racism," a collection of theories extent in Western society about the multiple meanings of "race" and whether "race" matters, and if so, under what circumstances, and to whom.

C12. Different professional specialties may form about those defined meaning sets which have the common (but not necessarily complete) assent of their practitioners. Widespread agreement on these "general" constructions does not render them "true," but it does increase confidence in their sense-making utility because of
 ̗¹   ͵h level of sophistication typically involved.

      ιlity of constructions shared among individuals (includ-
      ͵ssionals such as academics and scholars) occupying
       surround can be characterized as the culture of that
      hn's (1967) disquisition on paradigm shifts in science

is especially useful in considering how academic disciplines form and coalesce around a shared set of constructions, and how those constructions guide how science is pursued, how paradigm-breakers are "disciplined," and how crises in the disciplines lead to new constructions and new models of how science should be or could be pursued.

C14. Parallel constructions may be devised independently in different local contexts; such parallels are not necessarily evidence of their prior sharing or of generalization, or of scientific generalizability.

D—Knowledge

D1. Knowledge is the organized remembrance of experience; it is based in the first instance on the "realization" of primitive experiences and on the sense made of those experiences.

D2. Individual knowledge is the end product of sense-making, in the form either of a construct or a construction. Knowledge may of course be recorded as an *aide-memoire* and for the purpose of transmission. (This is one of the major purposes of colleges and universities: the collection, preservation, and transmission of a culture's knowledge.)

D3. Shared knowledge consists of the cumulative reconstructions of individual constructs or constructions (individual knowledge) coalescing around (tending toward) consensus.

D4. Knowledge, whether individual or shared, is advanced by continual testing by additional experience, by the assimilation of new experience (which may be vicarious), or by mental manipulation of primitive constructs or constructions into new forms which need not necessarily reflect experience (creation).

D5. Knowledge is always context-bound (and often that context is local); thus, knowledge is changed when the context is changed (context being range of experience and observation invoked in the knowledge construction, frequently in a familiar surround).

D6. Mentally formed (that is, created without the intervention of new experience, for example, *gedankenexperimente* in the sense that Einstein used the term) advanced knowledge can lead to seeking out experiences which the newly formed advanced knowledge suggests (a parallel to the development and testing of hypotheses).

D7. The search for such suggested experience may be interpreted as the search for empirical verification.

Please note here that empirical verification can exist as a physical reality (number of classrooms in an elementary school), or as a mental reality (for example, some teachers appear to be biased toward calling on boys in class rather than girls, even though girls tend to make better grades). The use of the term "empirical" has come to mean, in some quarters, only physical realities, or statistical representations of such realities. This particular construction of the term "empirical" is termed "rank empiricism"; indeed, empirical facts can exist as either physical realities or mental constructions (for example, racism, ageism, ableism).

D8. Nevertheless, empirical verification cannot be taken as evidence for the "true" existence of the devised construct or construction, but only for the internal consistency and integrity of the construct or construction itself.

D9. Knowledge, whether primitive or advanced, is not cumulative in the sense that prior elements form a sure foundational base for later added elements; instead, *knowledge accumulates in the form of ever more informed and sophisticated reconstructions.*

D10. Accumulated knowledge relevant to some particular area of professional interest and expertise may be termed disciplinary knowledge.

D11. Expertise may be characterized as thorough acquaintance with some area of knowledge together with experience in applying and/or extending that area of knowledge.

D12. All knowledge, whether primitive, individual, shared, advanced, or disciplinary, is continually open to challenge, which may lead to extension, modification, reconstruction, or abandonment, but never to the achievement of a foundational or ultimate truth.

D13. Shared knowledge acquiesced in by an interacting group of individuals, all of whom are willing to accept it, in the main, as representing their own constructs or constructions, or the best that is known at the moment, is the basis for their joint inquiry and action programs.

E—Dependence and Voice

E1. If epistemology is defined as transactional and subjectivist, then putative facts cannot be independent of the prior constructions held by the observer. This construction-dependence on facts is an inescapable consequence of the constructionist view. This observation holds for theory as well, since theories are also constructions.

Please note, too, that this is a compelling reason for the maintenance of a reflexive journal on all inquiries pursued by constructivists: to come to know, continually, the nature and shape of prior constructions, including most especially those which are held tacitly, and which may be previously unknown to the inquirer. Reflexive journals are a formidable tool—providing they are returned to on a regular basis both in the field and back from the field—for granting insight into constructions held but not previously recognized. Such journals are a means for coming to know the human as instrument, and for bringing to light prior constructions.

E2. Conversely, constructions (including theories) can never be fully determined by recourse to factual or empirical evidence. Pluralist views faithful to and accounting for the same putative "facts" are common. This indeterminacy of constructions (their unacceptability or incompleteness) is an equally inescapable consequence of the constructivist view.

E3. Under these circumstances, the voice that is "heard" in any construction is necessarily that of the constructor. If the constructor is a member of a "privileged" class, say, a scientist, then the construction, say, science, necessarily consists of the consensual voice of those privileged to be class members, say, other scientists.

E4. Every construction resonates to the values projected by the voice that shapes it; every construction is devised in the framework of the social, cultural, historical, political, economic, ethnic, and gender positions of the constructor.

E5. This state of affairs raises the question noted by Yvonna Lincoln (1993 address to the International Society of Clinical Psychologists) concerning the authority by which social scientists speak for "the Other." "This crisis of representation—the question of who the 'other' is, what partial picture of her/him is presented, who has the right to present that picture, and what the claims to both authority and authoritativeness are—is a formative question for postmodern social science."

E6. This issue in turn raises the question of legitimation: By what right does an inquirer make statements about others (putatively representing their views, culture, condition, and so forth), especially about those others who do not have access to power structures that may be making policy decisions that directly impact on their lives?

E7. Another issue of voice has to do with the forms of representation available to the others by means of which they can state their own positions and beliefs (present their own constructions). If the forms of representation are limited, by virtue, say, of schooling, of socialization, of enculturation, or of powerlessness, available constructions are limited, truncated, or invisible.

This situation is partly resolved when inquirers take into collaboration their research participants, training them to gather data and to contribute as full partners in the representations which are made. In some contemporary instances, inquirers cannot even enter a site without a co-researcher's being assigned from among those "native" to that site. In this manner, local research participants at least partially control the representations which are made of them, have the power to nominate issues, claims, and concerns that are critical to the local context and that require that at least a portion of the inquirer's time be spent on issues which concern local residents, rather than focusing solely on academic and researcher interests (Lincoln & Denzin, 2005, 2011).

E8.   These issues and dilemmas can only be resolved (partially, if at all) by a consensual construction arrived at through negotiation with all interested and concerned parties, a negotiation which hears and honors all voices and takes them fully into account.

    In some instances, because of value conflict at the inquiry site, consensual constructions cannot be negotiated. In this instance, both (or all) sides should have their positions fully and fairly represented in any and all reports.

F—Paradigms

F1.   Efforts at large scale, higher level, complex sense-making ultimately rest upon sets of basic beliefs (presumptions) within which the efforts can be organized, expounded, rationalized, and defended.

    CAVEAT: Rationalizing a construction does not necessarily imply that one follows the rules of classical logic, whose utility is widely questioned and whose nature is being challenged by the existence of "alternative logics," the most unconventional being so-called "fuzzy logic" (Kosko, 1993).

F2.   These overarching sets of beliefs, together with their putative implications, may be described as *paradigms*. Constructivism is one such paradigm; the passages included herein are such implications.

F3.   Paradigms rest upon the most fundamental sets of beliefs that can be enunciated by their proponents. They cannot be justified on any more external, objective, or foundational grounds; if they could, then those grounds would assume the status of the most fundamental beliefs. Ultimately the proponent of any paradigm is forced to the admission that he or she believes what is believed because he or she believes it, however self-referential that may be.

F4.   Paradigms need not be, and often are not, commensurable; that is, they may not be reducible to a common set of standards by which inconsistencies or conflicts among them can be resolved. Choices must then be made; accommodation is often impossible.

    CAVEAT: It may be the case that commensurability is more likely if constructions are cast in non-verbal forms, or if alternative forms of logic, for example, fuzzy logic, are utilized in the test for commensurability. It may also be possible to deal with apparently incommensurable paradigms by negotiating a metaparadigm which subsumes them and makes their inconsistencies irrelevant. To date, such a metaparadigm has not appeared.

F5.   If individual constructions are found to be commensurable, they are most likely grounded in the same paradigm.

F7.   If different paradigms are found to be commensurable, they are most likely reducible to a common set of first principles, belief systems, or presumptions. This might be the case, for instance, in examining the constructivist paradigm alongside the participatory/action research paradigm, or in comparing the constructivist paradigm to certain models of a criticalist paradigm.

F8.   Consensus can be achieved within paradigms but not between incommensurable paradigms, except by negotiation which renders its precursors irrelevant (but not untrue).

Nevertheless, even though consensus cannot be achieved between incommensurable paradigms, incommensurable paradigms might be able to extend and amplify the knowledge (or constructions) produced in one by knowledge (or constructions) produced in another. This is an argument frequently advanced by proponents of so-called mixed methods designs, and it is not without some merit. This is, however, an *additive* function, not a consensual function.

F9.   Successful paradigms tend to persist until new information can no longer be reconciled with (or subsumed under) the paradigm's presumptions, or until questions arise which cannot be elegantly answered by the original (successful) paradigm. In fact, it is most often troubling questions which lead to the proposal of a new paradigm, since the old one is unable to address new questions which arise in any meaningful way.

F10. The most heuristic paradigms will most rapidly lead to their own replacement.

G—Inquiry

G1. The aim of inquiry is the achievement of continuously improved understanding and extended sophistication, which is accomplished through the reconstruction or extension of existing constructions and/or the development of new constructions.

G2. There are three distinct but often confused forms of inquiry: Research, evaluation, and policy analysis.

  a. *Research* is a form of inquiry whose focus is some proposed or existing knowledge construction and which is aimed at the extension or revision of that construction (reconstruction) and/or the development of related new constructions. Knowledge reconstructions and the development of related constructions are sense-making efforts built upon formal assessment of available or obtainable information using the most sophisticated discovery and assimilative techniques that are applicable. Basic research results in theoretical knowledge constructions; applied research results in practical knowledge constructions.

  b. *Evaluation* is a form of inquiry whose focus is some *evaluand* (the program, process, organization, person, and so forth being evaluated) and which is aimed at the development of "merit" and/or "worth" constructions (value judgments) about that evaluand. Merit constructions converge on the innate quality of an evaluand, irrespective of the setting in which it may find application. Worth constructions converge on the usefulness or applicability of the evaluand in a concrete local situation. The evaluation of a proposed or developing evaluand is termed formative, while the evaluation of some developed evaluand is termed summative.

  c. *Policy analysis* is a form of inquiry whose focus is some proposed or existing policy (guide to discretionary action, mandated practical action, legislation, or legal/juridical decision) and which is aimed at the extension or revision of that policy construction and/or the development of new policy constructions. Such constructions are always value judgments, which can be informed by research or evaluation but can be *formed* only by bringing value judgments to bear, whether explicitly or implicitly (Lincoln & Guba, 1986).

Which value judgments, representing which stakeholders, under what circumstances and in what contexts, is a political matter. Indeed, most policy analyses are attempted to analyze and provide critique of proposed and/or existing policy, with the aim of extending the policy, re-targeting the policy, reformulating the policy, or overturning the policy. Many contemporary policy analyses are undertaken for the purpose of determining their impact on some segment of society, for example, women, African-Americans, Hispanics, or gays, that might find itself discriminated against or otherwise impoverished or disadvantaged by virtue of the policy.

G3. Inquiry is a conscious, systematic, and disciplined sense-making effort intended to develop, and expected to lead to, a more informed (inclusive of more and perhaps different meanings) and/or more sophisticated (more complex, higher level and/or larger scale) construction than is currently available of some focus—something of which we may need or wish to make sense. The new construction may be devised *de novo* or may be a more informed and sophisticated reconstruction of an existing one. The latter change may range from simple inclusion of an additional item of meaning or higher level of sophistication to a complete paradigm shift.

G4. A problem is some aspect of a selected focus that imposes a barrier to sense-making at some point in the evolution of the needed or desired construction or reconstruction, and thus calls for inquiry. The barrier may initially be more "felt" (tacit) than "realized," and may therefore require extensive rationalization before it can be stated in constructed (propositional) form.

G5. Problems are characterized by two or more elements (propositions) juxtaposed to highlight an apparent knowledge gap, inconsistency, conflict, or paradox. The juxtaposed elements may be drawn from within a single construction or between or among commensurable constructions.

Problems in social science tend to fall into three categories: action problems, conceptual problems, or value problems. In action problems, inquirers (and frequently practitioners) are confounded by not knowing what to do. In conceptual problems, inquirers are not certain what to believe, particularly about two conflicting sets of research, or two conflicting models (think, phonics versus whole-language reading instruction). In value problems, researchers are unclear which set of values might be most critical in a social issue (consider the value conflicts between freedom, equity, and efficiency).

G6.   Different paradigms are likely to highlight radically different problems; indeed, what is a problem in one paradigm may not be so considered in another (and may not even be able to be articulated in the terms of another paradigm).

However, just because a problem cannot be sensibly articulated in another paradigm does not render it moot. Rather, it suggests that elements of the issue at hand are being viewed from another perspective, or that thinking is occurring "out of the box," or that issues arose in its application which were unforeseen in the development of the original theory/program/module, or the like.

G7.   Inquiry has two phases or stages:

a. Discovery: An effort to describe "what's going on here," the "here" being the focus, and its context, to which the problem pertains. The discovery phase may not be needed (or may be needed only minimally) if there is a pre-existing construction or constructions relating to the focus on which to build; that is, if some meanings and some level of sophistication are already available. There are many ways in which the discovery question can be answered, depending on what specific relevant and pre-existing constructions are brought to the inquiry by the inquirer and by local informants (respondents). Discoveries are themselves also semiotic organizations, that is, mental constructions.

CAVEAT: If the pre-existing constructions are drawn from the literature, care must be taken in their assessment to ascertain their paradigmatic bases; if those bases are not lodged in constructivism, serious disjunctions could easily be overlooked. In fact, many fruitful discoveries have resulted from a paradigm exploring an issue that the same or another paradigm believed already settled by utilizing constructivism. Engaging in such inquiry often leads to new insights or findings which conflict with, or contradict, the original findings.

b. Assimilation: The process of incorporating new discoveries into the existing construction or constructions (or, if the discovery is sufficiently different from or in conflict with the existing construction or constructions, replacing them) so that the "new" (more informed and sophisticated) construction will fit (subsume older and newer meanings), work (explain what happens), demonstrate relevance (enable the core problem to be resolved, ameliorated, or better defined), and exhibit modifiability (be itself open to change).

G8. Discovery and assimilation are not necessarily sequential processes, but may overlap or be carried out in parallel.

G9. Both discovery and assimilation can be carried out using the hermeneutic/dialectic methodology (see H). In this methodology, competing (conflicting, contradictory, or non-isomorphic) constructions are examined in ways intended to move them toward some common consensual construction. If no common consensual construction can be found, findings might be labeled anomalous and temporarily set aside. When disciplines confront too many anomalies (anomalous findings which are non-isomorphic with existing constructions), according to Kuhn (1967), a crisis occurs, and eventually a new paradigm is proposed which subsumes both the classical constructions and the anomalies.

G10. In most inquiry, the inquirer is likely to hold a different construction (or even a different paradigm) from those persons most closely related to the object of inquiry, loosely called respondents or members. The former view is conveniently labeled the *etic* (or outsider) view, while the latter is conveniently called the *emic* (or insider) view.

G11. Since the inquirer's view is almost certain to differ from the insider's emic view, the intrusion of an inquirer into a local context will necessarily disturb and disrupt it, another aspect of the "social Heisenberg effect."

G12. The fit between metaphysics (paradigmatic presumptions) and phenomena is more critical than is usually believed. If the inquirer's paradigm construction differs from that of the local context and culture, inquiry findings may appear to insiders to be irrelevant and unpersuasive precisely because of the lack of paradigmatic match.

H—Hermeneutic/Dialectic Methodology

H1. Methodologies appropriate for some inquiries may not be useful, and may even be dysfunctional, for others. Each paradigm sets its own methodological requirements. All methodologies, however, should be carefully fitted to the ontological assumptions of the paradigm. In other words, the strategies for seeking knowledge of some set of realities should be commensurate with how those realities are defined.

H2. If a selected methodology does not exhibit a high degree of "fit" with the phenomenon studied and with the paradigm within which that phenomenon is defined, useful sense-making cannot result.

H3. While there are three distinct types of inquiry—research, evaluation, and policy analysis—the hermeneutic/dialectic methodology is appropriate to all. The sought-after constructions differ among these three types, but the means for developing these different constructions are identical.

H4. Hermeneutic/dialectic methodology is carried out via a series of encounters between and among inquirer and respondents (inquiry participants) focusing on their initial constructions and aimed at developing reconstructions by a process in which all share equally.

H5. Hermeneutic/dialectic methodology begins with the establishment of circles of respondents (often called hermeneutic circles) within which various constructions can be juxtaposed and examined in an encounter format.

H6. Hermeneutic circles are formed of small groups of respondents so as to reflect the composition and interests of various stakeholder (at-risk or affected) groups, one circle for each such group. Gatekeepers are especially useful for identifying individuals who should comprise each group.

H7. Reflecting the two stages of constructivist inquiry, the hermeneutic/dialectic methodology has two products:

ο a. Descriptive constructions (of focus and surround):

  1) Varying descriptive constructions (of knowledge, evaluand, and/or policy, depending on the type of inquiry) are elicited in turn from the several individuals (respondents) in each circle in a non-judgmental context. These constructions may have both qualitative and quantitative elements. This step constitutes the main but not the only hermeneutic element in the total process.

  2) Each individual is then asked, again in turn, to comment on the constructions of the others in his or her own circle, indicating why, having heard the others, they now prefer those other constructions (or aspects of other constructions) or continue to prefer their own. Their stated reasons become part of the negotiation process. This step begins the dialectic portion of the process, the encounter.

  3) After a number of iterations, a consensual construction will probably begin to emerge, although it is not likely that full consensus will ever be achieved.

 b. Assimilative constructions (of focus and surround):

  1) Varying assimilative constructions are developed in each circle based upon and drawing from the consensual (or nearly so) descriptive constructions that have been devised in the *other* circles. These are carried iteratively around the hermeneutic circles until a consensual construction emerges (or comes as close to emerging as possible), or

until it begins to be obvious that no consensual construction will be possible, due to fundamental value conflicts between stakeholders and inquiry respondents. This step is again primarily hermeneutic in nature, although dialectics plays a role, principally because of this occasional inability to come to a consensual construction.

NOTE: As Western society becomes more pluralistic and diverse, it seems likely that consensual constructions will not frequently be arrived at. In this instance, dialectics takes over, and it may be more fruitful to portray the value conflicts underlying non-consensus constructions.

2) Other constructions may be drawn from lay and professional literature, from the inquirer's own knowledge and experience, from existing documents (local and elsewhere), and from observations, and be introduced into the circles for consideration.

CAVEAT: Of course not all such related constructions (especially those drawn from the professional literature) will rest on constructivist principles, and hence must be evaluated carefully. But these other constructions may be examined simply as competitor constructions, evaluated for their relevance, and included in whole or in part as appropriate. This step is primarily dialectic.

3) The process criteria of increased/increasing knowledge and/or sophistication, and of fitting, working, demonstrating relevance, and exhibiting modifiability, are utilized throughout.

4) Negotiation is the process key, as constructions are compared and modified in the direction of consensus. Even when consensus is unable to be reached, negotiation between stakeholders holding conflicting constructions can prove useful, enlightening, and enlarging of potential constructions. Thus, negotiation always has a role to play, even if its only task is to demonstrate to stakeholders where and in what ways their constructions are incompatible.

5) The inquirer as human instrument is pivotal in achieving the desired descriptions, for there is no other information gathering and/or analyzing mechanism that can deal directly with the mental constructions of others or orchestrate the negotiation.

H8. The hermeneutic/dialectic process both deconstructs and reconstructs (every construction is a reconstruction). The initial constructions drawn from stakeholders, from the literature, from documents, from observations, and from the inquirer's own experience are analyzed so that their terms of meaning, points of similarity and contrast, and omissions may be noted. Once this deconstruction has occurred, it becomes possible for participants to reconstruct a new, joint construction which will, for all parties, be superior in level of meanings and degree of sophistication to any of the initial constructions, as well as fitting, working, demonstrating relevance, and exhibiting modifiability.

CAVEAT: It will sometimes be the case that participants (respondents) will construct a new construction, but there will be several of them, rather than a single, joint construction. See H7 for a brief discussion of how conflicting value systems may prevent a consensual construction. They do not, however, prevent new, emerging, and more sophisticated reconstructions on the part of stakeholder groups.

H9. Deconstruction is aimed at disassembling the discourse structures, reifications, myths, metaphors, artifacts, and practices found in a construction in order to lay bare the assumptions which undergird its production, employment, and deployment.

H10. Deconstruction can easily become elitist (consider, for example, the phrase, "erasing false consciousness"), thereby undermining the negotiation process. The ground rules must make clear that the ultimate intent is achieving consensus, not merely sharpening differences (although the latter may be the only achievable goal at a given point in time).

H11. If the initial constructions differ, among other ways, in that they are based upon different paradigms, consensus will not be possible unless the stakeholders can agree on a common paradigm, or the discussion can be moved to a superordinate paradigm level, that is, a paradigm that makes the earlier paradigms jointly irrelevant (a move that at the moment defies explication).

H12. The methods for achieving the descriptive and assimilative products of the hermeneutic/dialectic methodology are primarily qualitative in nature, since it is only the human instrument that can engage in the interviewing, observing, analysis of documents and records, negotiation, and the like—all qualitative techniques—essential to uncovering and reconstructing existing constructions of focus and surround. However, quantitative methods will also be widely used whenever appropriate, as, for example, an element of a construction, in numerical description of entities involved in the inquiry, in providing substantiating evidence for some claim, and in other ways. Constructivists do not eschew quantitative methods unless those methods are inconsistent with constructivist presumptions, as, for example, causal path analysis because it assumes causality chains that a relativist ontology explicitly rejects. Both propositional and numerical discourse are admissible.

H13. The success of the hermeneutic/dialectic methodology is, paradoxically, dependent on the existence of a minimal level of resistance and conflict that must be resolved to achieve a common construction. Total consensus cannot (fortunately) ever be achieved, for if it were, communication would cease, the groups that had initially held different (or competing or conflicting) constructions could no longer function as communities, and the forces holding the communities together would disappear. (See also K4.)

H14. The emergent constructions (the current shared meanings) will remain in play until the appearance of new meanings (meanings which add to or challenge some elements of meaning within the construction) and/or increased sophistication (such as the appearance of a new statistical or qualitative analytic technique) leads to reconstructions, which are again tested with the hermeneutic/dialectic methodology.

—Quality Criteria

I1.   The quality (rigor) criteria for an inquiry cast in relativist ontological terms, in transactional/subjectivist epistemological terms, and in hermeneutic/dialectic terms must be appropriate to such a paradigmatic framework; they cannot be objectivist or foundational.

I2.   Whatever criteria emerge, they must also reflect the moral, ethical, prudential, aesthetic, and action commitments of constructivism.

I3.   It is proposed that the quality of the hermeneutic/dialectic methodology, and thus of the outcome of a constructivist inquiry, be determined by bringing to bear certain criteria called authenticity criteria, none of which can be considered to be foundational:

   a. *Fairness* is determined by an assessment of the extent to which all competing constructions have been accessed, exposed, deconstructed, and taken into account in shaping the inquiry product, that is, the emergent reconstruction(s).

   b. *Ontological authenticity* is determined by an assessment of the extent to which individual constructions, including that of the inquirer, have themselves become more informed and sophisticated, or the extent to which individuals themselves become aware of constructions that they did not realize they held until the inquiry brought them from the tacit to the propositional level.

   c. *Educative authenticity* is determined by an assessment of the extent to which individuals, including the inquirer, have become more understanding of, more sophisticated about, and more tolerant of the constructions of others.

   d. *Catalytic authenticity* is determined by the extent to which action (clarifying the focus at issue, moving to eliminate or ameliorate the problem, sharpening values) is stimulated and facilitated by the inquiry.

   e. *Tactical authenticity* is determined by an assessment of the extent to which individuals are empowered to take the action that the inquiry implies or proposes.

I4. Methods for making the quality assessments defined in I3 include:

a. For fairness: informed consent procedures; prolonged engagement and persistent observation by the inquirer; *prior* explication of the inquirer's etic position; individual and group member checking; use of a peer debriefer and post facto auditor by the inquirer.

b. For ontological authenticity: dialectical conversations; openness of purpose; explication of inquirer's etic position; caring and trusting relationship with respondents; comparison of respondents' and inquirer's initial and final personal constructions; respondents' and inquirer's introspective statements about their own growth.

c. For educative authenticity: dialectical conversations; use of peer debriefer and auditor by inquirer; comparison of respondents' and inquirer's assessments of the constructions held by others; respondents' and inquirer's introspective statements about their understandings of others' constructions.

d. For catalytic authenticity: development of a joint construction (aiming at consensus when possible), including the assignment of responsibility and authority for action; respondent/inquirer collaboration; accessibility of final report to all stakeholders; evidence of practical applications.

e. For tactical authenticity: negotiating data to be collected, their interpretation and their reporting; maintenance of confidentiality; use of consent forms; dialectical conversations; member checking; inclusion of representatives from all at-risk groups as respondents; prior agreements about power; training in accessing the corridors of power, if necessary.

J—Application

J1. Constructions are necessarily based on local circumstances and experiences, and hence have applicability, strictly speaking, only in the local situation.

J2. Not all persons in a local setting will necessarily share a construction; holders of competing constructions may be intermingled in the local setting (milieu, surround, community, culture).

J3. Nevertheless, constructions, as they may be formulated at any given time or as reported in a case study, may find application in new, non-local contexts or may be adapted by holders of competing constructions in a local setting, in any of the following ways (CAVEAT: this statement should not be understood as legitimizing generalization; the concept of generalization has no meaning in the terms of the constructivist paradigm):

a. Constructions may be shared with members of other contexts who accept, for whatever reasons, the given constructions as appropriate in their contexts (that is, they reconstruct their earlier constructions to accommodate the newly adopted constructions, or they discover findings and constructions useful in their own situations or contexts).

b. Imported constructions may provide vicarious experience which can guide further inquiry or action in the same ways that actual experience does. Such vicarious experience can be provided at both propositional and tacit levels (the latter because case studies can invoke affective and intuitive, as well as cognitive, responses).

c. Imported constructions may generate "working hypotheses," propositional statements which may be examined for possible meanings in the new contexts.

d. Imported constructions may serve as metaphors, stimulating new ideas and insights in contexts which are metaphorically parallel. Metaphors appeal to human imagination; without imagination it would be impossible to escape from conventional constructions into alternatives.

e. Imported constructions may serve to test the receivers' own constructions; in effect, the receiver may carry out a personal hermeneutic/dialectic, testing his or her own local constructions in relation to the new construction(s).

J4. Malconstructions—that is, constructions which overlook available meanings, facts, or evidence, or fail to utilize appropriately sophisticated analytic techniques—can be formed by virtue of ignorance or sloth, although it is likely that such would be quickly challenged and disposed of in the hermeneutic/dialectic process.

J5. Malconstructions can also be formed when not all persons engaged in a hermeneutic/dialectic interchange do so in good faith, or from a position of integrity. Deliberate malconstructions intended to deceive or manipulate (for example, in the case of political "spin doctors" who propose constructions which put their candidate in the best possible light) are not unlikely in situations in which one or more of the stakeholders is placed at serious risk.

CAVEAT: In situations in which malconstructions of this deliberate type may occur, the quality criteria outlined earlier may be insufficient to establish the meaningfulness of any emergent construction. If good faith cannot be assumed, the inquiry becomes even more political in nature than it might otherwise be (see L3c and I1).

K—Change

K1. Constructions, once articulated and shared, become stabilized and are quickly reified to become part of the socio-cultural milieu or surround.

K2. Reified constructions are a powerful force in support of maintaining the status quo. If the underlying paradigm (implicit or explicit) provides a warrant for believing the construction to be "true," the construction is virtually impervious to change; it becomes effectively foundational.

K3. Faced with an effectively foundational construction, participants (especially novices and learners) have no choice but to learn what that "truth" is. There are no exceptions or contraventions. Certainty precludes discussion; truth is coercive.

K4. There cannot be personal or social progress in the face of "truth" defined a priori. Progress requires that there be differences to explore, challenges to meet, conflicts to resolve, and ambiguities to clarify.

K5. Persons persist in maintaining existing constructions when they see no alternative.

K6. The most powerful leverage to change an existing construction is obtained by challenging its constructor with difficulties, conflicts, and/or ambiguities that can no longer be reconciled with that construction. Lack of certainty leads to reconstruction.

K7. Reconstruction begins with deconstruction; the effort to analyze discourse structures; myths, metaphors, artifacts (music, film, art); and practices to illuminate the presumptions that undergird their production, employment, and deployment.

K8. Individual change occurs when dissonance between the individual's personal construction and the challenging elements grows so great that continuing to hold to the original construction becomes rationally and emotionally impossible.

K9. Large scale change occurs whenever there is sufficient agreement among a group of disaffected constructors on some new construction to warrant action and the group is sufficiently motivated to undertake it.

K10. The de facto change agent is an instrumentality—a person or entity such as a speech, tract, film, and so forth—who or which brings the challenging elements to the attention of holders of older constructions.

K11. Since it is the inquirer's responsibility to orchestrate the hermeneutic/dialectic process, the inquirer is de facto cast in the role of primary change agent.

L—Ethics and Politics

L1. Every human institution and every human action, including inquiry, is both profoundly ethical and profoundly political in nature.

L2. Ethical problems can arise in several ways in constructivist inquiry:

a. Participants, both observers and respondents, may deliberately introduce malconstructions, as noted above. The hermeneutic/dialectic process is itself probably the best, but sometimes not a complete, safeguard against such deceptions.

b. The inquirer may fail to set up the traditional safeguards: maintaining confidentiality, obtaining fully informed consent, guarding against harm, and protecting privacy. Such safeguards can probably best be provided through review by "human subjects committees," which in turn attend to both legal and professional (as in codes of ethics) requirements.

There are, however, problems with human subjects protection committees themselves. In the current political climate, frequently institutional review boards (IRBs) become interested more in protection of themselves and their universities, and less able to make judgments which reflect sound assessments of the proposed research (Lincoln & Tierney, 2004). In other instances, they act as regulatory agents, forcing interpretivist, constructivist, or other predominantly qualitative work into a different paradigmatic mold, thereby inactivating the very premises on which the original research was proposed, or acting to push qualitative work into conformity with (inappropriate and meaningless) regulatory ideals such as those proposed by the National Research Council (2002; see, for instance, Cannella & Lincoln, 2004; Lincoln & Cannella, 2004, 2009).

c. The constructivist inquirer may (or better yet, will) face special ethical challenges: face-to-face contact makes privacy and anonymity within a site or research location difficult to maintain; the need for trust is high but trust is difficult to achieve and easily shattered, and frequently must be re-earned at regular intervals in a research context; the nature of the case study report almost precludes confidentiality, at least with respect to knowledgeable locals, since adequate description leads to sensible deductions regarding who is speaking. Furthermore, it is more often than not the case that arguments repeated verbatim in case reports will have already been shared in other venues between stakeholders long before the researcher enters the context.

These safeguards can be attained only through intensive personal contact and attention, and can never be guaranteed. Participants must at all times be kept apprised of such risks, most especially at the beginning of any inquiry as one of the elements included in the fully informed consent contract. Participants must have the right to withdraw from the inquiry at any time, and receive all data collected from them back into their hands.

d. A special challenge which the constructivist inquirer does not face is the tilt toward deception which characterizes many non-constructivist inquiries. Deception is sometimes justified on the ground that if the respondent knew what the inquirer was "really after," he or she would not be forthcoming. Thus, it is asserted, the inquirer is warranted in keeping his or her "true" purpose hidden from the respondents, in the name of uncovering some more valid knowledge or serving some higher social good. But since constructivism deals with the constructions that respondents have "realized" in their minds, to deceive them about the purpose of the inquiry would not only be unethical but absolutely counterproductive to the aim of eliciting descriptions and attempting assimilations.

L3. Political problems can also affect inquiry in a variety of ways:

a. Since there is no objective reality against which to test any construction, every construction will speak with a certain voice, reflecting the knowledge, sophistication, and values of the person or persons (inquirers and respondents) who devised the construction in the first place.

b. In some instances, constructions will speak with a "new" voice, in the sense that the knowledge/understandings/constructions therein will be actually *co-constructions*, or knowledge, understandings, and the like generated collaboratively by the inquirer and respondent. The respondent may have never considered an issue until it is raised by a researcher, and consequently, must formulate a response on the spot. This new knowledge is, in fact, a co-constructed form of knowledge (Karnieli-Miller, Strier, & Pessach, 2009), and thus a blend of the researcher's curiosity and the respondent's attempt to deal with a puzzling/intriguing issue never encountered previously. Much constructivist inquiry is built around these co-constructions, such that the "realities" presented as findings are, in fact, new understandings of the world on the part of both inquirer and research respondent.

c. Since inquiry cannot be shielded from the impact of values held either by the inquirer or by the respondents, every act of inquiry is simultaneously a political act, in the sense of the exercise of power.

We cannot say enough about the influence of power in the research setting, and the uses, abuses, and unspoken ramifications of power are some of the most thoughtfully and extensively explored issues in interpretivist and constructivist inquiry (and indeed, in positivist inquiry also, although many positivists deny there are any power issues in their work [Baez & Boyles, 2009]). Karnieli-Miller, Strier, and Pessach (2009) argue that there is a significant "tension" generated between the ideals of qualitative inquiry toward democratization of the inquiry process and the authority and relative power of the traditional researcher, which raises both "multiple ethical dilemmas and serious methodological challenges" (p. 279). Indeed, achieving non-manipulative and authentic, collaborative relationships in the field is one of the ongoing issues with constructivist and interpretivist inquirers and ethnographers (Bravo-Moreno, 2003; Ceglowski, 2000; Collins, Shattel, & Thomas, 2005; Duncombe & Jessop, 2002). Power is the fulcrum of these ethically tangled relationships (Ebbs, 1996), and politics its constant companion (Baez & Boyles, 2009).

d. The voice reflected in any inquiry report cannot carry greater privilege than any other; to act as if it did is coercive and disempowering of those who may not have had input into its formulation but may nevertheless be at risk.

One means for avoiding the "voice from everywhere, the voice from nowhere" is to work with research participants as co-constructors of the research questions and issues, and to work with them as co-authors of any and all final reports, publications, or other written work. A multi-vocal text provides less opportunity for privileging one voice over another, one perspective above those of others.

L4. Constructivist inquirers have a special obligation, given these ethical and political considerations, to take a posture of advocacy and activism with respect to all stakeholder groups with which they interact, particularly those that are in some way disempowered.

A special case exists, however, for stakeholder groups who elect not to become research participants, but who determine, as a group, that they will stand outside the research process and wait to speak until "the results are in." No researcher, of course, can force the participation of any respondent or stakeholder group, but special efforts must be made to involve them early on, if at all possible.

L5. Since constructions are all influenced by the voice(s) of the constructors, the constructivist inquirer must arrange the hermeneutic/dialectic process so that all voices can be heard and honored; that is, the constructivist inquirer must practice advocacy (on behalf of all stakeholding groups).

L6. Similarly, the inquirer must do everything possible to ensure that the joint construction that emerges is acted on; that is, the constructivist inquirer must practice activism (if action elements are included, as for example, but not solely, in an evaluation).

L7. The ultimate moral imperative for the constructivist is to be not only open to new information or levels of sophistication that challenge the construction currently held, but actively to seek them out and to take them into account.

It is also the case that a moral imperative exists (we hesitate to rank it) to work, wherever possible, for extended social justice (Kahn, Mastrioanni, & Sugarman, 1998; O'Connor & O'Neill,

2004; Strier, 2007). This is another arena in which there is developing an extensive, broad, and rich literature as constructivist and qualitative researchers confront the ethical demands of a recaptured, reconceptualized and recommitted form of research vastly differentiated from the objectified demands of the "culture of science" and scientism. The use of inquiry to extend democratic and participatory ends—a teleological mandate—counters the "taming" effects of the regulatory ideal embedded in "science" as proposed by proponents of experimental methods.

M—Case Reports

M1.   The typical form for the presentation of inquiry reports has been text and numbers. Nowhere is this state of affairs better illustrated than in professional journals, which are, as Eisner (1993) has suggested, "encomiums to technical language." Other forms of representation (film, photos, poetry, plays, readers theatre, media montages, various kinds of performances, and others) are needed.

M2.   The report of a constructivist inquiry is most usefully made in the case study format (which can incorporate any of the above alternative forms), as a re-presentation of the multiple constructed realities fashioned via the hermeneutic/dialectic discourse, because:

a.   The case study format delivers sufficient scope and depth to afford vicarious experience (including tacit vicarious experience), sufficient understanding to suggest working hypotheses, sufficient richness to point to useful metaphors, and sufficient detail (usually in the form of thick description) to permit a reader to test a personal construction, all of which are important means to facilitate application in other, non-local settings. Please notice that application to other contexts is not a decision made by the researcher/inquirer, as would be the case in positivist inquiries, where the researcher makes a statistical estimate of generalizability. Rather, transfer to other contexts (that is, transferability) is a decision which can only be made by a potential user. It is, however, the responsibility of the original researcher to provide sufficient detail about the context, actors (participants), context-embedded (community and program) values, and context processes for intended users to understand whether or not there might be sufficient likeness between contexts to make findings for context number one useful in a second (or multiple) context(s). Thus, transferability takes the place of generalizability as a criterion for making a judgment regarding rigor in constructivist studies.

b. The case study provides the thick description needed to apprehend, appreciate, and understand the circumstances of the setting, including, most importantly, its physical, social, economic, and cultural elements.

c. The case study is perhaps the only format that can remain true to the moral imperatives of constructivism, that is, to serve as a credible representation of the various local constructions encountered and of any consensus construction (if such can be attained) that has emerged; that can adequately identify and reflect the voice or voices that influence the outcome; that can enlarge the understandings of respondents while at the same time serving the purposes of the inquiry; and that can stimulate and sustain local action by respondents (for which the inquirer acts as orchestrator and facilitator) as well as in other sites through the medium of the case report's readers.

M3. Case reports should be presented in ways that lay bare the metaphysical, aesthetic, rhetorical, political, and axiological conditionality of the constructions that they realize. One implication of such a case study is that it reveals at the deepest level possible (given time, resources, and other limitations) various values which inhere in the context.

M4. Case reports should reflect the shift in mode of discourse appropriate to the constructivist paradigm, viz:

a. From foundational truth-telling about "how things really are and really work" to relativist sense-making via one or more consensually constructed realities;

b. From generality to local understanding;

c. From accretion of knowledge to contextual sense-making;

d. From a we-they (inquirer-subject) polarity to an etic-emic fusion from which all parties profit; and

e. From the stance of detached observer or voice of a stranger to the passionate participant deeply involved in the reconstruction of a "reality" in which all, including the inquirer, have a stake.

M5. The goodness or quality of the case report **itself** must be judged by criteria appropriate to a presentation rather than to the inquiry process itself. These include:

a. *Axiomatic* criteria that demonstrate the resonance of the inquiry report with the basic belief system of constructivism:

1) Ontological relativism: by honoring multiple realities, displaying etic and emic views, however many, and avoiding generalizations and cause-effect statements or implications.

2) Epistemological transactionalism: by displaying and clarifying values, by celebrating subjectivity, and by identifying clearly the voice or voices that permeate and shape the report.

3) Methodological hermeneutic/dialecticism: by detailing in a separate methodological appendix or addendum the entire process followed in collecting and interpreting information.

b. *Rhetorical* criteria that demonstrate good writing style and persuasive argumentation, including:

1) Unity, that is, advancing some or only a few central idea(s).

2) Good organization.

3) Simplicity and clarity (especially to be accomplished through the use of "natural language").

4) Craftsmanship: demonstrating power, elegance, egalitarian values, and the writer's own emotional and intellectual commitment, as well as values; and retaining an open and problematic posture.

c. *Action* criteria that demonstrate a commitment to change and action:

1) Fairness: open- and even-handed treatment, with no information withheld from any stakeholder group.

2) Educativeness: for both inquirer and respondents.

3) Actionability and empowerment: identifying needed action as well as the impediments to it; pressing for the empowerment of those who must take action.

d. Although Schwandt (1996) has warned us that we must say "farewell to criteriology," constructivist research is often attacked on the grounds that it is not rigorous, or that it fails because of its inherent subjectivity. We would point out that there are actually *two* sets of criteria by which such inquiries might be judged: *methodological* criteria and *intrinsic, or paradigmatic fidelity* criteria. While we attended to those briefly earlier, it seems useful at this point to recollect them for the reader. Fuller explanations of these criteria can be found in Guba and Lincoln (1981, 1989) and Lincoln and Guba (1985).

1) Methodological criteria: plausibility, transferability, dependability and confirmability (which takes the place of internal validity, external validity/generalizability, replicability/reliability, and objectivity, respectively).

2) Intrinsic/paradigmatic fidelity criteria: fairness, ontological authenticity (an individual process), educative authenticity (a group process), catalytic authenticity, and tactical authenticity.

Part 3

Constructivist Conjectures
At Work

One of the things suggested as useful to do would be to take a real case study and note where constructivist conjectures and thought processes were at work. For this example, I (Lincoln) chose a recent dissertation. It was particularly well done, and located some findings that should have been far more widely discussed than they were. Elaine Linell Demps (PhD, Texas A&M University, 2008) most graciously assented to having portions of her third (methodology) and fourth (findings) chapters utilized to demonstrate how some of the conjectures worked themselves out in her own research.

In the sections which follow, I have reprinted her chapters on the right, and my own assessment of the constructivist assumptions, pre-sumptions, and conjectures on the left. Some readers may disagree with me, and that is their perfect right. Nevertheless, I am fortunate in that I have had the benefit of many conversations over time as the research, analyses and drafting of this work took place, and feel confident that I can represent both the writing which appears here and my own tacit and propositional knowledge carried over from dissertation meetings among Dr. Demps, Dr. Susan Lynham (chair of the dissertation com-mittee), and myself.

The Constructivist Credo, by Yvonna S. Lincoln and Egon G. Guba. 83–198

Some background would likely be useful for the reader. The dissertation is titled *Understanding the Faculty Experience of Teaching Using Educational Technology at Public Research Universities in the Academic Capitalism Era: An Interpretive Critical Inquiry.* Ten faculty members at two different institutions gave time and energy to explain their perspectives on teaching with technology—the benefits and the downsides. While it is clear that research universities have a great stake in encouraging faculty to utilize technology more widely, particularly in providing online courses and programs (which are billed at a different rate from in-class, face-to-face teaching rates), it is not always clear that those same universities provide the support systems necessary to both maintain and sustain faculty efforts in this virtual environment. Faculty satisfaction is tightly tied to both the departmental or university technical support provided and their own pleasure in learning new technology and teaching with it. Several faculty admitted that their interest in, and utilization of, high-tech teaching technologies drew time and energy away from the kind of activity which is more often rewarded than is good teaching—attracting external funding to support research publication. One or two of them ruefully admitted that they knew they would never make full professor because of the energy expended in teaching with technology, including "time constraints, steep learning curves, technical problems, and…pedagogical challenges" (Demps, "Abstract"). The latter references, among other things, the intellectual challenge of taking face-to-face material and transforming it into an online format.

Demps considers the contradiction between teaching with technology—and the enormous time that it takes to do it right—and fulfilling the mandates of a university caught up in academic capitalism. Critical issues are raised regarding whether faculty should concentrate on good teaching, and suffer the consequences for their own professional careers, or respond to the mandates for acquiring external research funding, ignoring the messages about putting more and more courses online. In true critical fashion, Demps points out that the university cannot do both and do them well. The investment of time and pedagogical thought which goes into teaching with technology simply precludes other university priorities for these faculty.

Excerpts from Elaine Demps

Understanding the Faculty Experience of Teaching Using Educational Technology

This chapter details the methodology for this study. The overview of the five components that comprise methodology—theoretical paradigm (Denzin & Lincoln, 2005), research strategies, participant and site selection, data collection and analysis, and trustworthiness—are provided as well as the specific methodology for this study.

G10[1] **Theoretical Paradigm**

Paradigms are "overarching philosophical systems" (Lincoln, 2005, p. 230) or a paradigm is "the net that contains the researcher's epistemological, ontological, and methodological premises" (Denzin & Lincoln, 2005, p. 22). The theoretical paradigm that guides conventional inquiry is positivism; interpretive or naturalistic inquiry is interpretivism or constructivism; and critical inquiry is critical theory (Denzin & Lincoln, 2005; Guba & Lincoln, 2005; Lincoln & Guba, 1985).

---

1. It is not clear whether the researcher holds a different (etic) paradigmatic view from her participants, but she makes every effort to begin to lay out her assumptions so that both readers and her participants, if they are interested, can be clear regarding what her etic view is shaped by, and what her research values are. This is an ethical stance regarded by most constructivist, interpretive, and/or critical researchers as absolutely necessary for any piece of research.

Geertz predicted more than 10 years ago that the different genres, or paradigms, would blur, and his forecast has come true (Guba & Lincoln, 2005). Guba and Lincoln state "indeed, the various paradigms are beginning to 'interbreed'" (p. 192) and inquiries (Denzin & Lincoln, 2005; Guba & Lincoln, 2005; Lincoln & Guba, 1985) can be guided by multiple paradigms: "a personal example is our own work, which has been heavily influenced by action research practitioners and postmodern critical theorists" (p. 192).

This section first provides an overview of the three paradigms—positivism, interpretivism, and critical theory—that can guide an inquiry. This overview serves as a rationale for the subsequent discussion on why a blended genre of interpretive critical inquiry was selected as the theoretical paradigm for this study.

G10[2]   *Positivism, Interpretivism, and Critical Theory*

Given that a paradigm is a philosophical system comprising ontology, epistemology, and methodology (Denzin & Lincoln, 2005; Lincoln, 2005), three paradigms—positivism, interpretivism, and critical theory—will be described and contrasted by their underlying ontology, epistemology, and methodology. In addition, each paradigm's axiology will be described since axiology is also a part of the philosophical system (Carpenter, 2002).

Ontology, or "theories of reality" (Lincoln, 2005, p. 230), poses the question *What is reality?* (Carpenter, 2002; Ruona, 2000). Epistemology, as a study of the nature, source, and validity of knowledge, poses the question *How do we know?* Methodology, also known as strategy of inquiry, is the approach to carrying out an inquiry, and includes the "assumptions, principles, and procedures" (Schwandt, 2001,

---

2. Here, Demps assumes that not all readers might share her paradigms and paradigmatic assumptions, and also that they might not be familiar with what those paradigms represent in philosophical or metaphysical terms; the next few sections attempt to create a statement of the etic view which will frame both her research and analytic efforts.

p. 161) that guide the researcher (Denzin & Lincoln, 2005). Inquiry, a word that refers to "a quest for knowledge, data, or truth" (*American Heritage Dictionary*, 2000, para. 3) is synonymous with research, and "research is an orderly investigative process for the purpose of creating new knowledge" (Swanson, 2005, p. 4). Examples of methodology are case study, ethnography, phenomenology, grounded theory, life history, action research, and clinical research. Axiology, comprised of ethics and aesthetics, addresses how values come into play in an inquiry (Carpenter, 2002; Lincoln & Guba, 1985).

Positivism

Attributed to the French philosopher Compte as having coined the term, positivism is a form of naïve realism (ontology) and naïve empiricism (epistemology) that applies the scientific method (Guba & Lincoln, 2005; Merriam, 1991; Schwandt, 2001). Naïve realism refers to an ontology that there is one reality or world external and independent of our minds which can be studied in individual parts (Lincoln & Guba, 1985; Schwandt, 2001). Naïve empiricism states that the world can be objectively studied through the experiences of the senses: observation and experiment. Scientific method, also called the hypothetico-deductive method, tries to explain human behavior through nomothetic, or lawlike, generalizations that follow a process of (a) forming theory-based hypotheses, (b) logically deducing predictions about the human behavior that will be observed, (c) testing the predictions through empirical observations, (d) concluding whether the theory explains the behavior or not (consistent or inconsistent with the facts measured), and (e) based on the results of the observations, keep, discard, or modify the theory (Schwandt, 2001). The assumption of positivism is that an inquiry can be carried out without the influence of a value system (axiology) (Lincoln & Guba, 1985).

Interpretivism

Rooted in various fields and philosophies such as hermeneutics, semiotics, phenomenology, symbolic interactionism, and the Chicago school of sociology, interpretivism emerged as a paradigm with an ontology, epistemology, methodology, and axiology opposite of positivism (Carr & Kemmis, 1985; Denzin & Lincoln, 2005; Lincoln & Guba, 1985; Merriam, 1991; Schwandt, 2001). Interpretivism opposes the positivism's ontological view that there is one reality, external to the mind, and capable of being studied in parts. Instead, interpretivism proposes a relativist world of multiple realities that are constructed and co-constructed by the mind(s) and required to be studied as a whole. Rather than the objective facts that are measured by the researcher, interpretivist epistemology seek out subjective beliefs that are co-created between the researcher and the researched, where the "knower and known are interactive, inseparable" (Lincoln & Guba, 1985, p. 37). Interpretivism aims "to replace the scientific notions of explanation, prediction and control, with the interpretive notions of understanding, meaning and action" (Carr & Kemmis, 1986, p. 83). The methodologies typically carried out in interpretive inquiry include those ideal for coming to understand the lived experiences of the researched. These methodologies include case study, ethnography, participant observation, phenomenology, ethnomethodology, life history, and historical method. The assumption regarding axiology in interpretivist inquiry is value laden.

Critical Theory

Many thinkers have helped shape the paradigm of critical theory. Those frequently cited include the German philosophers Hegel, Marx, and the Frankfurt School (Horkheimer, Adorno, Marcuse, Benjamin, Fromm, and Habermas) (Merriam, 1991; Schwandt, 2001). However, other philosophers and theorists such as Foucault, Derrida, and Freire have also helped shape the paradigm (Kincheloe & McLaren, 2005). The main tenet of research based on critical theory is the emancipation of those researched by making aware of their oppression based on social, cultural, political, economic, gender, sexual, ethnic, or racial values (Guba & Lincoln, 2005; Merriam, 1991; Schwandt, 2001). To bring about emancipation, the researcher engages in dialogues with the researched, and in praxis, the socially conscious action that emerges and becomes enmeshed with the ways of living of the researcher and those researched. The ontology is historical realism, "virtual reality shaped by social, political, cultural, economic, ethnic, and gender values, crystallized over time" (Guba & Lincoln, 2005, p. 193). The epistemology is subjectivist, formed between the researcher and the researched, and aims for emancipation from the oppression. The methodology is dialogic, and axiology is more than value laden, in that the inquiry is prompted and guided by the researcher's values.

Interpretive Critical Inquiry

Interpretive critical inquiry, then, draws from both the interpretive and critical theory paradigms, is an example of Geertz's blurred genres, and could be seen as a response to the criticism that interpretivism's aim of coming to understand the lived experiences of the researched stops short of questioning how their world is so and what can be done to address any social conflict in their world: "In particular, it is argued that the interpretive model neglects questions about the origins, causes and results of actors adopting certain interpretations of their actions and social life, and neglects the crucial problems of social conflict and social change" (Carr & Kemmis, 1986, pp. 94-95). Therefore, interpretive critical inquiry is a form of interpretive inquiry carried out with praxis or social change as a goal. The following characteristics are also inherent in the interpretive critical inquiry (Guba & Lincoln, 2005; Lincoln & Guba, 1985).

1. Aim of inquiry is not to generalize but to develop working hypotheses.

2. Cause-effect relationship is impossible as human behavior is embedded in context and time.

3. The researcher is the human instrument, guided by the ethics of not marginalizing the researched in any way (Guba & Lincoln, 1981).

4. Knowledge formed provides vicarious experience.

5. Trustworthiness, authenticity, and catalyst for action form the criteria for judging for quality and goodness (Guba & Lincoln, 1989).

Theoretical Paradigm and Rationale for This Study

The underlying theoretical paradigms of my study were interpretivism and critical theory, and thus, the inquiry was interpretive critical. The rationale behind the blurred genre of interpretive critical inquiry will be explained from the perspective of human resource development (HRD) and from the experience of conducting a pilot case study on understanding the faculty experience.

Rationale from the HRD perspective. Everything about HRD involves people. The domains of outcome comprise people (e.g., individuals, groups, organizations) (Swanson & Holton, 2001); the HRD professionals are people; the work carried out involve changing people (e.g., HRD as organizational change agent/interventionist, organizational empower/meaning maker, developer of human capital [Watkins, 2001]). While there may be situations when conducting a conventional inquiry would be appropriate (e.g., did the hard drives of the computers of one department that were turned off at the end of a day crash less than those of another department whose computers were not turned off?), for the most part, interpretive inquiry may be more amenable to inquiries in HRD because the widgets in HRD are humans whose behavior cannot be predicted or controlled and who are themselves context and time sensitive (Lincoln, 2005; Lincoln & Guba, 1985).

The questions I raised concerning teaching using technology were not about *counting* how many faculty members had adopted educational technology or *measuring* whether or not teaching using technology was more effective for students than teaching traditionally without technology. While these may be valid questions for some, I was more interested in learning about the lived experiences of faculty as they tried

to teach using technology. I assumed there would
realities, where one faculty member's experienc
different in some way from another. I was not str
objective truth but expected through subjective transactions
between me, the human instrument, and the faculty members,
the researched, we would co-create some understanding which
could be used to inform meaning and desired action. I was
not aiming to generalize the findings, or provide cause-effect
explanations, but rather, to provide enough thick description
to make transferability possible (Lincoln & Guba, 1985).

Rationale from the pilot case study perspective. The need for a
critical perspective was determined from a pilot case study I
conducted for a research course on naturalistic inquiry which
I completed as part of my doctoral coursework. From conducting that pilot case study, I came to understand that faculty can
experience much anguish and can feel burdened by teaching
using technology. Even those faculty members who believed
that educational technology could be an effective learning
resource and cognitive tool, and have therefore adopted it,
were hampered by the social system of the higher education.
For example, when faculty are typically rewarded for research
and publication efforts, more so than their teaching (Sutton &
Bergerson, 2001; Hearn & Holdsworth, 2002), and teaching
using technology is a time-consuming process, what parts of
the system of higher education need to be changed in order
to accommodate or encourage those who want to teach using
technology? Is the system oppressing the faculty—a highly
educated workforce—by expecting them to teach using technology but not rewarding (or worse, penalizing) them for the
time spent doing so? Attending to these questions appeared to
require a critical approach.

Research Strategies

The two research strategies for this study were social phenomenology and ethnography. Social phenomenology, attributed
to Schutz, is aimed at providing the explanations for how we

produce and experience our ordinary daily lives (Schwandt, 2001). Ethnography is a strategy for "describing a culture" (Spradley, 1980, p. 3). Together, these research strategies guided me in trying to understand the culture of public research universities and how the faculty members produce and experience the daily lives of teaching using educational technology.

M2b[3]   Site Selection

The research sites were two public research universities, University A and University B, of one system of higher education located in the south central region of the US. Based on the latest Carnegie Classification system that uses the enrollment figures of the fall 2004 semester (The Carnegie Foundation for the Advancement of Teaching, 2007), University A is a large, comprehensive doctoral research institution with an enrollment figure of around 40,000. University B is a majority graduate, professional, and special-focus institution with an enrollment figure of around 1,000. Both universities are located in the same city, a growing college town of population greater than 80,000. Based on this city government's website, more than 50% of the residents 25 years old or older earned at least an undergraduate degree.

University A

Founded in the last quarter of the 1800s, University A is a land-grant institution with 10 colleges ranging from agriculture, architecture, business, education, engineering, to liberal arts. Ranked by the Carnegie Classification system as a research university, its annual research activities exceed $500 million (The Carnegie Foundation for the Advancement of Teaching, 2007). Based on the Fall 2006 semester figures available from the website of the university's institutional studies and planning office, the total number of tenured or tenure track faculty was 1929. Those on non-tenure track were 858.

---

3. The role of thick description

The average age of the assistant professors was 37.7, associate was 48.5, and full was 57.5. The average age of non-tenure track faculty was 45.8. The faculty members were predominantly male: 77.6% male and 22.4% female. In terms of faculty race or ethnicity, University A was a predominantly white institution. The institution's Fall 2006 data available at its website categorized the tenure-track faculty in this manner: 74.4% were white, 2.7% were black, 4.9% were Hispanic, 8.1% were Asian, 0.3% was American Indian, and 9.5% were international.

Of the total number of undergraduate, masters, Ph.D., and professional students during the Fall 2006 semester, the race/ethnicity distribution was 73.6% white, 3% black, 10.9% Hispanic, 3.8% Asian, 0.5% American Indian, 7.8% international, and 0.5% unknown or other. The gender distribution was 47.3% female and 52.7% male.

University B

Unlike University A, University B provided much fewer facts and figures at its website. Thus, the amount of data to report regarding University B was smaller than those reported on University A.

According to the facts found at the University B website, it was officially established in the 1990s as a health professions university. Although it has been in existence as a consolidated entity for only a decade or so, some of its components have been in existence for a longer period. For example, its dental school was founded in the early 1900s and its medical school was founded in the 1970s. Today, University B comprises six schools or colleges and two centers. Of these components, two are located in the same city as University A. One of the two was a research site. The remaining six components of University B are located throughout the south central region state.

University B's most recent annual report was based on the 2005 data. According to this annual report, University B employed a total of 1,199 faculty members across the six schools and colleges; a total of 1,169 students were enrolled in the six schools and colleges.

Participant Selection

The participants were selected based on purposive sampling and were faculty members on tenure track who were actively engaged in teaching using educational technology. My aim was to invite faculty members who were faced with the conflicting demands of academic capitalism (i.e., to be productive awardees of externally funded research grants) and teaching using educational technology (i.e., an endeavor riddled with many barriers). I planned to start with a pool of 10 faculty members as study participants and continue the process of contacting more faculty members until the assessment of the emerging richness of the data indicated no further participants were needed (Lincoln & Guba, 1985). Indeed, collecting data from the 10 study participants did generate a rich set of data and no further participants were needed.

Purposive sampling is a method of identifying study participants who are chosen based on extreme cases, typical cases, maximum variation cases, critical cases, politically important cases, or convenience sampling (Patton as cited by Lincoln & Guba, 1985). The criteria for purposive sampling I used for this study included extreme, critical, and politically important cases. Extreme cases are those that are "particularly troublesome or enlightening" (Lincoln & Guba, 1985, p. 200), critical cases are those that allow "maximum application of information" (Lincoln & Guba, 1985, p. 200) because information elicited from critical cases are such that other cases will also yield similar information, and politically important cases are those that can bring attention to a study. These three criteria seemed appropriate for identifying faculty who were faced with the conflicting demands of academic capitalism and teaching using educational technology. Thus, I invited faculty members who were committed to teaching using educational technology and whose perceptions included (a) a large amount of time devoted to preparing educational technology course materials (extreme case), (b) a rich experience of teaching using educational technology (critical case), and (c) an experience of an adverse consequence as a result of their commitment to teach using educational technology (political case).

Participant Selection Process

I began identifying the possible participants before I received the Institutional Review Board (IRB) approval of my research study so that I might immediately begin to collect the data when I received the approval. I identified the possible participants through the help of two service units at University A: the teaching excellence unit and the instructional technology support unit. My dissertation committee co-chairs and committee members suggested contacting these two service units as a starting point because the staff there would be aware of faculty members who taught using educational technology at both University A and University B. I emailed either the director or associate director of both units and was provided with 23 names of potential participants. In addition to the 23 leads, I planned to invite two faculty members who had participated in my pilot case study for the naturalistic inquiry course.

Reviewed Faculty Status

Once I received the names of the 23 potential participants, the next step in carrying out my purposive sampling criteria was to check to see if they were tenured or on tenure track. I used University A's directory of faculty, which also provided information about the faculty from University B, to check the titles of the potential participants. I considered the faculty whose titles were assistant, associate, and full professors as being on tenure track or tenured. I considered those whose titles started with *Clinical* (e.g., clinical associate professor) or whose titles indicated a staff position (e.g., *Director*) as non-tenure track. This process yielded 14 tenured or tenure-track faculty members. The interesting point at this stage was the lack of assistant professors who were on the list. Of the total 23 names recommended, only one was an assistant professor.

Emailed Invitations

I had a pool of 16 (14 suggested names plus my two prior case study participants) faculty members to invite. However, I emailed an invitation to 15 faculty members; I omitted one potential participant by error and did not discover this oversight until I started to analyze the data. Of the 15 I invited, one faculty member informed me that he was not on tenure-track. I was not sure of the tenure-track status of his *Lecturer* title so I had invited him. Another one indicated that he may be able to participate but he did not participate after all. Four responded that they would participate. Eight did not respond at all.

Attended Users' Group Meeting

I attended a users' group meeting of a course management system (e.g., Blackboard, Moodle, and ANGEL) available to both University A and University B. I was able to speak briefly about my research study and distributed a flyer with my contact information. Speaking about my study at this meeting resulted in three additional participants who fit my purposive sampling (two accepted my invitation at the meeting and one of the two referred a third one).

Visited University A's Distance Education Website

I visited University A's distance education website to learn about programs that may be delivering their courses using educational technology. I emailed the faculty of programs I found at the website. This effort yielded two additional faculty members.

Asked Participants to Suggest Potential Participants

During my interviews, I asked the participants to suggest other potential participants. This approach yielded one additional participant.

Total Participants

Table 16 lists the total number of faculty members, 10, who participated in my study. The table lists each participant's pseud onym, university affiliation (University A or University

B), title, gender, race/ethnicity, and how I recruited the participant. They are listed in the chronological order in which I interviewed them.

Data Collection

The data collection occurred over an 8-month period between April and December 2007. The three methods of data collection used for this study were (a) ethnographic interviews, (b) participant observations, and (c) document analyses. The ethnographic interviews took place between May and June 2007, the participant observations took place between April and May 2007, and the document analyses took place between April and December 2007.

An *ethnographic interview* is a method of collecting data from study participants by carrying out conversations with explicit purposes (Spradley, 1979). The researcher starts by asking questions intended to build rapport with the participant and subsequently asks questions to elicit information about the participant's culture. *Participant observation* is the process of engaging in the typical activities of a social situation with the purpose of observing the people and activities of the situation (Spradley, 1980). *Document analysis* involves obtaining documents and records appropriate for a study and analyzing and interpreting the data obtained from them (Schwandt, 2001). The specifics of how these three data collection methods were used for this study are described in a subsequent section.

Ethnographic Interviewing

Once I received the IRB approval to start my data collection, I scheduled the interviews. At each interview meeting, I provided the participant with the IRB approved information sheet about my study prior to launching the ethnographic interview. The interview lengths ranged between 40 minutes and one hour and 50 minutes; the average length was approximately one hour and 10 minutes. I interviewed eight participants in their offices and two at a neutral location. The two participants were interviewed at a neutral location because, initially, I thought our IRB regulations required the interviews to take place away from the participants' office. However, a phone call to the IRB office revealed that I could interview the participants in their office. Therefore, eight were interviewed in their office.

Recording the Interviews

The interviews were audio recorded on two devices, a Sony® microcassette tape recorder and a Sony® digital recorder with 256 megabytes (MB) of built-in memory. As a backup to the audio recordings, I also handwrote the interview conversations in my interview journal. The drawback of writing down the conversations was that I was so absorbed in capturing the participant words that I neglected to record my observer's comments. In hindsight, writing the interview conversations seemed to have been overly redundant. However, I did find that the act of writing down the conversations yielded an unforeseen advantage: a forced pause. Later, as I listened to the audio recordings to transcribe the interviews, I realized the conversations were interweaved with very brief segments, around 15 seconds or less, when I was busy writing and the participants were waiting for me to finish. This waiting period seemed to have resulted in a forced pause allowing the participants to perhaps think further on what they had just said because after I finished writing, they often delved deeper and elaborated on the point they had just made. Therefore, in my future research studies, I plan to take handwritten notes as a pause-tool for helping the participants to reflect, but rather than writing the interview conversations, I may record my observer's comments. More details on the process I used to transcribe the interviews will be described in a section below.

Interview Protocol

Not surprisingly, of the three data collection methods, the interviews produced the most illuminating data because as a human instrument, I was able to ask, probe, and tailor the interviews in a manner appropriate for each participant as well as my research questions. Although I followed an interview protocol with three sets of predetermined questions, I allowed the unfolding conversation with each participant to sequence the order in which the questions were asked.

Transcribing the Interviews

The Sony® digital recorder I purchased, model ICD-P520, came bundled with the software Digital Voice Editor version 3.0. I found this software very helpful in transcribing the interviews. After each interview, I connected the digital recorder to my laptop using a Universal Serial Bus (USB) cable and used the voice editor software to copy the interview recordings on the digital recorder to my laptop hard drive. I placed each interview file in a separate folder on my laptop. Since these interview files were in a proprietary format, as a safety measure, I also created a copy of the files in an MP3 format, a more universal audio file format that can be played back on many common audio devices such as a CD player.

One of the functions in Digital Voice Editor 3.0 was *Transcribing*. Once an interview file was copied to my laptop, I selected that file and pressed the Transcribing option. Digital Voice Editor would display a text editor, Windows Notepad, as well as a tool bar containing the start, stop, pause, fast forward, and rewind buttons. Most of these tool bar functions were also accessible by using the keyboard function keys. In addition, Digital Voice Editor provided a feature to slow down the playback speed to as slow as 75%. Thus, the transcribing process entailed listening to the interviews from my laptop with an ear-bud headphone at a slowed down playback speed of about -30%, typing what I heard directly into Windows Notepad, and pressing the functions keys F11 to stop and F10 to restart, and CTRL and left or right arrow key to incrementally rewind or fast forward, respectively. Being a very slow transcriber, I found the voice editor a helpful tool. After transcribing the fifth interview or so, I was able to transcribe at a rate of approximately five hours for every hour of interview conversation.

Phases in Transcribing the Interviews

I followed a 3-phase process in transcribing the interviews. The first phase was using the Digital Voice Editor to create a

Windows Notepad file containing the almost verbatim interview conversation. This file was almost verbatim because I omitted filler words such as *um* or *uh*. The second phase entailed converting the Windows Notepad transcript file into a Microsoft Office Word file. Once converted into a Word file, I checked for misspelled words and added a header that included on the left-hand side a participant's pseudonym, interviewee number, interview date and time and on the right-hand side the page number of the interview transcript. I considered this second phase file a *pure file*. The third phase was when I reviewed the Word interview transcript from the second phase and changed most of the identifying information such as names and places. For example, when a participant said the actual name of University A, I changed that actual name to *this university*. Or, when a participant mentioned a colleague's name, I changed that name to a pseudonym or to *a colleague*. I also edited for obvious grammatical errors that can occur in the spoken English language such as verb tense mismatch or singular/plural noun and verb mismatch. However, in one case, I did not change an interviewee reference to two countries, Spain and Japan, as places she grew up because disguising those countries in that context made the resulting text meaningless. I considered this third phase file the *final transcript* for conducting member-checking and for analyzing the interview data.

Participant Observation

The purpose of the participant observations was to allow another perspective for collecting the data (Lincoln & Guba, 1985) on how the participants teach using educational technology. During the spring and summer 2007 semesters, the period when I conducted the interviews and participant observations, some participants used educational technology to supplement their face-to-face class meetings (Interviewees #1, 3, 4, 5, 7, and 10) while others taught strictly online (Interviewees #2, 6, 8, and 9). Of the six participants who met with their students face-to-face, I was able to observe a class meeting of three (Interviewees #3, 5, and 10). I kept field notes of the participant observations in order to record the details of my experience of the observations as well as to record what I saw during the observations (Emerson, Fretz, & Shaw, 1995). In addition to the classroom observations, I obtained a guest account to review Interviewee #3's supplemental course website. Of those who taught strictly online, I obtained access to review three course websites, those of Interviewee #2, 6, and 8. These participant observations will become useful in *Chapter IV, Data Analysis and Results,* when what I observed will be included as thick descriptions (Geertz, 1973).

Document Analysis

Pertinent documents of the study participants and of University A and University B were sought, reviewed, and analyzed for another perspective on the data (Lincoln & Guba, 1985). For example, documents such as the course syllabi, faculty curriculum vitae, college policies and procedures manual, and institutional facts were reviewed as well as informative external documents such as the Carnegie Classifications (The Carnegie Foundation for the Advance of Teaching, 2007). The process I used involved looking for facts that either served to fill a gap or confirm the interview data. For example, one faculty member was not sure of the year he became tenured and suggested I review his curriculum vitae available on the Web. Doing so allowed me to find the exact year. As another example, I retrieved and reviewed a college's policies and procedures manual to better understand the performance evaluation criteria of tenure-track faculty of that college.

Data Analysis

I analyzed the interview data using the content analysis technique as described in Lincoln and Guba (1985). The process I followed entailed five broad steps: (a) unitizing the interview data, or, identifying the individual units that subsequently are grouped into themes (Lincoln & Guba, 1985); (b) coding the units; (c) identifying the categories of similar units; (d) noting the emerging themes; and (e) subdividing the themes into subthemes. The specifics of this process are provided in the following paragraphs.

Unitizing the Interview Data

The sources for the unitizing process were the *final transcript.* In one case, the final transcript was slightly edited by a participant after he reviewed his interview transcript for the purpose of member-checking. The details on member-checking are provided in the *Trustworthiness* section later in this chapter.

My plan was to print the units of data on 5" x 8" index cards and comb-bind the cards on top. Therefore, I reformatted the source files from letter size (8.5" x 11") to 5" x 8". Then, I increased the font size from 12 points to 14 points for easier legibility and also increased the top margin to allocate space for comb-binding. I added a header that included the interview number, interviewee pseudonym, interview date, interview time, and the index card number. I also used Microsoft Word's line numbering feature to number each line to facilitate locating a piece of text at a later time, if necessary.

Once a final transcript was reformatted to fit the 5" x 8" index cards, I read through the transcript and created a hard page break whenever I identified a unit of data. This step resulted in separating the units of data by forcing a new unit to start on a new index card. However, because some units of data spanned multiple index cards, I added a visual demarcation using horizontal lines: one line was placed at the beginning of a unit, at the top of a card, and another line was placed at the end of that unit.

Coding the Units

Once all the final transcripts were unitized, I printed each transcript onto the 5" x 8" index cards and had the cards comb-bound at a local print shop, separated into interviews. My initial thought was to code the units by placing color-coded post-it notes on each unit within a comb-bound set of cards. However, my dissertation co-chairs predicted this method of coding would prove to be cumbersome and suggested I unbound the cards. I did.

After unbinding the cards, I reviewed each unit of data, wrote a short summary on a post-it note that served as a code, and affixed the post-it note to the unit. I continued this coding process until I coded the first five interviews.

Identifying the Themes

After coding the first five interviews, I paused to identify the emerging themes by grouping the index cards with similar codes or meanings. After grouping the cards of the first five interviews by similar codes or meanings, I placed each set of related units into a broad umbrella theme and planned to subdivide the broad theme after unitizing and categorizing the remaining five interviews.

Noting the Emerging Themes

Eleven broad umbrella themes emerged. I returned to the remaining five sets of interviews, coded the remaining index cards, and sorted the cards into the 11 themes. No new theme emerged from the last five sets of interviews.

Subdividing the Units in Each Theme

After all 10 interviews were unitized, coded, and categorized into the 11 umbrella themes, I returned to them and subdivided each umbrella theme into subthemes. These themes and their subthemes are listed at the end of this chapter and will be discussed in detail in the following chapter, *Chapter IV: Data Analysis and Findings.*

---

11   **Trustworthiness**

Trustworthiness refers to the quality of an inquiry—whether the findings and interpretations made are an outcome of a systematic process, and whether the findings and interpretations can be trusted (Lincoln & Guba, 1985). At least three sets of trustworthiness criteria have been offered: (a) Lincoln and Guba's criteria for trustworthiness, authenticity, and catalyst for action (Guba & Lincoln, 2005; Lincoln, n. d.; Lincoln, 1995; Lincoln & Guba, 1985); (b) Carr and Kemmis' (1986) four validity claims;

and (c) Lather's (1991) four validity criteria. In the following sections, the three sets of criteria are described first, followed by a rationale for selecting Lincoln and Guba's criteria for trustworthiness, authenticity, and catalyst for action as the appropriate trustworthiness criteria for this study.

M5c   *Lincoln and Guba's Trustworthiness, Authenticity, and Catalyst for Action*

The trustworthiness criteria are separated into two categories: a set of criteria termed "parallel methodologic criteria" (Lincoln, 1995, p. 277) that correspond to the rigor criteria of conventional inquiry and "authenticity/ethical criteria" (Lincoln, 1995, p. 277) "which took as their epistemologic basis the claims, concerns, and issues of the new paradigm" (Lincoln, 1995, p. 277). These two categories of trustworthiness criteria are illustrated below. The reference sources are Guba and Lincoln (2005), Lincoln (1995), and Lincoln and Guba (1985). Another reference source is a class handout (Lincoln, n. d.) from *EDAD 690N: Naturalistic Inquiry,* taught by Dr. Yvonna S. Lincoln, and the verbal explanations of the criteria she provided during class on November 22, 2005.

Credibility corresponds to the internal validity criterion of positivism and refers to establishing confidence in the findings and interpretations of a research study. The techniques for assuring credibility include prolonged engagement, persistent observation, triangulation of sources, methods, theories, and researchers, peer debriefing, negative case analysis, referential adequacy, and member checks.

Transferability corresponds to the external validity criterion of positivism. In the conventional inquiry, external validity or generalizability would be assured by measures taken (e.g., randomized controlled trial) to ensure that the findings will be applicable in different contexts or subjects. In interpretivism, generalizability is not an aim; instead, the applicability of the findings and interpretations is to be determined by those who want to apply the findings and interpretations. In interpretivism, this transferability is possible through thick description (Geertz, 1973), where the researcher provides enough description of the context so that the reader can determine whether the findings apply to his or her context.

Dependability corresponds to the reliability criterion of positivism and addresses how the findings and interpretations could be determined to be an outcome of a consistent and dependable process. A technique for achieving dependability is an audit where a designated person reviews the inquiry process as well as the "data, findings, interpretations, and recommendations" (Lincoln & Guba, 1985, p. 318) to check for consistency.

Confirmability corresponds to the objectivity criterion of positivism and refers to how the findings and interpretations are a result of a dependable process of inquiry as well as data collection. The techniques for assessing confirmability include an audit, triangulation, and reflexive journal.

---

13   Because the authenticity/ethical criteria are native to interpretivism, they do not correspond to the rigor criteria of positivism. Fairness refers to including the views of all stakeholders for a fair balance. Ontological authenticity refers to the researched learning something new about their social condition as a result of the research. *Educative authenticity* refers to facilitating the process of having the different sets of stakeholders learning about each other in order for the group to make an informed judgment. *Catalytic authenticity* refers to the findings of an inquiry serving as an impetus for social change or action. *Tactical authenticity* refers to the researcher serving as an agent of knowledge on how to bring about social change or action given the findings.

Carr and Kemmis' Four Validity Claims

Drawing on Habermas' thoughts on ideal speech situation, where those engaged in discourse can participate in "free and open communication" that results in democratic discussions for "emancipation from repressive distortions" (Carr & Kemmis, 1986, p. 142), Carr and Kemmis suggest four validity claims for speech: *truth* in what was said, what was said was *comprehensible, sincerity* of speaker, and *"right* for the speaker to be performing the speech act" (p. 141, emphasis in original).

Lather's Four Validity Criteria

Lather (1991) recommends four validity criteria for "praxis-oriented research … for research that is openly committed to a more just social order" (p. 66). The criteria are: (a) *triangulation* of sources, methods, and theories for data trustworthiness; (b) *construct validity* for building social theory for emancipation; (c) *face validity* through member checks; and (d) *catalytic validity* that facilitates the researched to take part in social change.

Trustworthiness Criteria for My Study

Lincoln and Guba's parallel methodologic criteria and authenticity/ethical criteria were adopted as the trustworthiness criteria because Lincoln and Guba's criteria are comprehensive and seemed to include most of Carr and Kemmis' and Lather's criteria. Table 18 details the actual techniques carried out for my study.

Triangulation of Sources

This trustworthiness technique refers to eliciting data regarding a topic from multiple sources of the same type in order to determine if different sources provide different information (Lincoln & Guba, 1985). For example, if ethnographic interviewing is the type of data collection method, asking the same question about a topic from different participants would be a triangulation of sources. I carried out this trustworthiness criterion whenever possible throughout the data collection process. The details of the findings will be described in the following chapter but as an example, when two participants were from the same department, I cross-checked the data gathered from one participant by asking the second participant a question about that piece of data.

Triangulation of Methods

This technique refers to using multiple forms of data collection to ensure accuracy of the data (Lincoln & Guba, 1985). By design, this research study used three forms of data collection methods: interviews, participant observations, and document analyses.

Triangulation of Theories

This technique refers to confirming a piece of data against multiple implicit and explicit theories (Lincoln & Guba, 1985; Y.S. Lincoln, personal communication, December 17, 2007). Although Lincoln and Guba (1985) initially considered this method of triangulation to be "epistemologically unsound" (p. 307), Lincoln's current thoughts are that researchers carrying out naturalistic inquiries do indeed triangulate their data against theories and this method can be used to ensure credibility.

I chose to confirm my data against two implicit theories and two explicit theories. The two implicit theories were: (a) teaching using educational technology is more effective than teaching traditionally without using educational technology; and (b) leadership support (e.g., department chair support) will help alleviate some of the first-order barriers (e.g., lack of technical support personnel) that confound teaching using educational technology. The explicit theories were: (a) human capital theory—economic gain can be achieved at the individual, organizational, or societal level as a result of investment in the human capital usually in the form of education and training (Becker, 1992; Sweetland, 1996; Schultz, 1961; Torraco, 2001); and (b) technology for social inclusion—attending to physical, digital, human, and social resources is necessary if technology is to be integrated meaningfully into society, or in the context of my dissertation study, into public research universities.

Negative Case Analysis

This technique refers to continuously adjusting the working hypothesis until a fair amount of outlying situations can be accounted for in the working hypothesis (Lincoln & Guba, 1985). For example, my findings seem to suggest that faculty members in departments that provide a strong educational technology support are less burdened by the technological issues of teaching using educational technology and seem to be able to focus on the pedagogical issues. Whenever relevant (e.g., when interviewing faculty members from departments with strong educational technology support), I asked a question directed at understanding where in this continuum of burdened-by-technological-issues and able-to-focus-on-pedagogical-issues a faculty member was.

Member Checks

This technique is where "data, analytic categories, interpretations, and conclusions are tested with members of those stakeholding groups from whom the data were originally collected" (Lincoln & Guba, 1985, p. 314). The end of the third phase produced the final *transcripts* that were deemed ready for the participants to review for accuracy of the content. I asked each participant to review the transcript to see if their thoughts were captured correctly, if I had hidden their identifying information well enough, and if they were satisfied with the pseudonym I had selected. I gave each participant between three and four weeks to review the transcript and asked each to send me any suggested changes. Of the 10 participants, one requested making changes that rendered him more anonymous, three responded within the allotted time with no change requests, and six did not respond. I consulted my dissertation committee co-chairs regarding the non-responders; their recommendation was to consider the non-responders as having approved their respective transcript.

I also sent the draft of *Chapter IV: Data Analysis and Findings* to the participants to provide them an opportunity to comment on the accuracy of how I described and quoted them as well as to decide if they wanted to omit portions of their quotes. I asked them to reply within 18 days and that I would consider those who do not respond as having approved their respective segments. Five participants responded and no one requested changes to be made.

Thick Description

This technique refers to providing enough details of the context of the research study in order to help a reader determine whether or not the findings are transferable to the reader's context (Lincoln & Guba, 1985). Thick descriptions were collected from the participant observations and document analyses, were introduced in this chapter when the research sites were described, and will be provided again in the next chapter, *Chapter IV: Data Analysis and Findings.*

Dependability and Confirmability Audits with Audit Trails

These techniques were carried out with my dissertation committee co-chairs; they were the auditors. The tools used were the fieldwork memo for data collection and the fieldwork memo for data analysis and findings. After the data collection, I met with my co-chairs and went over the fieldwork memo for data collection that detailed the data collection process. Similarly, a fieldwork memo on the data analysis and findings served as a tool for my co-chairs to conduct the audit on how I arrived at the results of the study.

E1   *Reflexive Journal*

This technique refers to keeping a journal in which the researcher carries out a conversation with herself or himself on topics related and not related to the research, as in a diary (Lincoln & Guba, 1985). The purpose of the journal is to keep a record of the changes occurring to the researcher—the human instrument and meaning-maker—both about the research and not. I have been writing in a reflexive journal specific to this research study since I began the data collection. I also have another reflexive journal which I began prior to commencing this study, while I was shaping the possible design of this study.

M5 *The Interviews*

I3b The interviews can be considered as the technique for satisfying the ontological authenticity. During some interviews, in responses to the questions I asked, participants seemed to experience an aha moment.

C7 *Publications Resulting from This Research Study*

Publishing the results of my research study could be considered a technique to satisfy the educative, catalytic, and tactical authenticities. If published, my findings may serve as a vehicle for social change or action either by institutions or by faculty. Toward this end, I plan to prepare and submit three manuscripts to peer-reviewed journals. One manuscript will focus on the implications of my study and findings for HRD, in particular, HRD's role in faculty and administrator development as well as in facilitating organization development in research universities. A second manuscript will target the educational technology community with the goal of informing both the scholars and practitioners the organizational forces resulting from academic capitalism (e.g., promotion and tenure criteria at research universities) that impede faculty adoption and implementation of educational technology into their teaching practices. A third manuscript will be intended for the higher education community and will be written to share the experiences of my study participants. Perhaps the readers who find the narratives applicable and relevant may begin a dialogue, within and across institutions, aimed at bringing about organizational change in research universities. More details about these anticipated manuscripts are provided in *Chapter V: Conclusions, Implications, and Recommendations.*

Summary of Methodology

This dissertation study was guided by the blurred genres (Geertz, 1973) of both interpretivism and critical theory and is thus labeled interpretive critical inquiry. The research sites were two public research universities, University A and University B, both located in one city in the south central region of the US. Using purposive sampling, I was able to recruit 10 study participants, tenured associate and full professors. I was not able to recruit any assistant professors on tenure-track. Data collection occurred over an 8-month period and made use of three methods: (a) ethnographic interviews, (b) participant observations, and (c) document analyses. The interviews were transcribed and analyzed using Lincoln and Guba's (1985) form of content analysis technique. The trustworthiness criteria selected were Lincoln and Guba's parallel methodological criteria and authenticity/ethical criteria (Guba & Lincoln, 2005; Lincoln, n. d.; Lincoln, 1995; Lincoln & Guba, 1985).

After analyzing the interview data, 11 themes emerged. They will be described in detail in the next chapter, *Chapter IV: Data Analysis and Findings.*

I have been waiting eagerly, yet anxiously, to write this chapter. Here is where I begin to share the stories—as they pertain to my research questions—of the 10 study participants and also offer some working hypotheses. As a beginner student of qualitative research, I recall a question I posed to my professor, Dr. Yvonna S. Lincoln, one evening after a class meeting of *EDAD 690N: Naturalistic Inquiry*: if the findings of qualitative research cannot be generalized, why do we bother to do qualitative research? Although the question was a follow-up to the content we had covered that evening, I carefully observed her expressions, concerned that I would be misunderstood as criticizing the methodology. Instead, I was genuinely curious and wanted to absorb her understanding of the topic. She paused for a fleeting moment—during which time I sensed that this question was often posed to her—and she replied graciously and excitedly: the end results of conducting qualitative research such as naturalistic inquiry are the working hypotheses that emerge and the narratives that tell the stories of some human condition from which anyone so inclined can learn (Y. S. Lincoln, personal communication, September 13, 2005).

That moment was an epiphany for me because I could intuitively relate to the value of narratives as data or findings. I was born in the US and spoke only English until my family moved to South Korea when I was four years old. Soon after moving to Korea, I became fluent in Korean but could no longer speak English. My journey to become fluent again in English was a painful and frustrating one because of the number of years the process required. It began with being enrolled in a first grade English as a Second Language (ESL) class at the Department of Defense Dependents School system I attended in Korea for the American military brats. Now I am bilingual, although English is my dominant language, and I have often wondered *which is my first language—English or Korean?* I have silently chuckled at my inability to answer that simple question with a one word response. Rather, the question seems to require a narrative. Therefore, that evening, hearing Dr. Lincoln's response energized and motivated me. That one response gave me the power to absolve forward all the critics of qualitative research whom I had yet to meet because the methodology made perfect sense to *me*. I also became hopeful that maybe one day I could serve as a messenger of the stories that make a difference to someone.

The remaining sections of this chapter are *Data Analysis*, *The Participants*, and *The Findings*. In *Data Analysis*, I will present a table listing the 11 emerged themes and their subthemes. In *The Participants*, I will introduce the 10 faculty members who volunteered to participate in my study. Finally, in *The Findings*, the three research questions will be addressed using the emerged themes and subthemes.

Data Analysis

After unitizing, coding, and categorizing the interview data, 11 major themes and multiple subthemes were identified. Table 20 below is included to remind the reader of the faculty members who participated in this study. All names are pseudonyms.

Table 21[4] presents the 11 major themes and the associated subthemes as well as the participant identifiers (i.e., the participant numbers I established according to the sequence in which I interviewed the participants) to relay who contributed with data that led to the emerged themes and subthemes.

The Participants

Carrying out this study was possible because of the 10 faculty members who volunteered to become study participants. I imagine many researchers, for one reason or another, experience difficulties in finding and recruiting participants and my experience was no different. Therefore, I am grateful to the 10 participants who chose to share a slice of their valuable time with me.

In this section, I will share what I learned about them as people—their attributes such as biographical data, courses they teach, teaching philosophy, motivation to pursue academia, or value system. The order in which I will introduce the participants will be chronological in terms of when they arrived at University A or University B. Up until this point, I have identified the participants in the sequence in which I interviewed them. The rationale behind the departure from that approach is to weave the participant introduction with the historical timelines of Universities A and B, whenever possible. Thus, the participants will be introduced according to the new sequence.

As you will soon notice, the lengths of the participant introductions vary. While some participants expounded on their biographical and professional background during the interviews, some did not. I respected those who chose not to share more of their personal information and did not probe for depth. Hence, their narratives will be shorter.

Jonathan Wilson, 1967

Jonathan Wilson belongs to a department at University A that is the "granddaddy of range departments anywhere in

---

4. Tables not included for reasons of space. The narrative covers this material.

the world in size, volume, and productivity" [Interview #4, card #155 of 175]. In fact, his affiliation with the department began in 1957, 11 years after the birth of the department, as an undergraduate student. Thus, his relationship with the department spans 50 years.

After receiving his undergraduate degree in 1961, Dr. Wilson went west for his master's degree; he earned it in 1963. He returned to University A in 1964 to start his doctoral studies. One summer of federal government work helped him to choose the academic career path:

> I worked one summer with soil conservation service, federal, between my junior and senior years in undergraduate, which helped me to decide that I didn't want to work for the federal government. I thought I was going that way career wise but I enjoyed my summer and I said that's not my career path. So that's when I switched over and began to pursue academia. [Interview #4, cards #35-36 of 175]

I asked him the reason behind the change in career path and he responded as shown below:

> The federal government is a top-down organization and very …. It's more where'd you spend your time and what records did you fill out than what did you actually do. I like the more entrepreneurial attitude of the academic environment in the university. They're not looking over your shoulder. They give you enough rope to hang yourself or make a ladder and climb out. It's up to you. [Interview #4, cards #36-37 of 175]

Dr. Wilson earned his doctoral degree in January 1968 but began working with the agricultural experiment station associated with University A in 1967. Then, he was located in the northern part of the state but in 1970 moved to the campus of University A as he began a joint appointment with the university and the experiment station. He received tenure and was promoted to associate professor around 1975 and was promoted to full professor in 1979.

Because Dr. Wilson has been a part of University A either as a student or faculty member for 50 years, he has seen and experienced many institutional changes. He recalled his undergraduate years and the total cost to earn that degree: "I completed my undergraduate degree on less than $1000 a year. Tuition, fees, room, board, total expenses. I completed my four years on less than $4,000" [Interview #4, card #76 of 175]. We attempted to calculate the present day value of $4,000, and based on the brand new Ford 2-door coupe he purchased for $2,500 upon his graduation, which we roughly estimated it to be equivalent to $25,000 today, we concluded that the cost of education has definitely risen since his undergraduate years.

The professoriate at University A also appears to have changed over the years. "In the '60s, tenure was almost automatic. It was not a very high bar" [Interview #4, card #33 of 175]. Furthermore, the university funding available for faculty research seems to have diminished over the years:

> My first 15 years with the System, my research was supported almost entirely by hard dollars through the system. By state dollars. It was about 1980 that we started looking out and saying "Oh we need to get grant funds." During the '70s we were beginning but very few of the faculty in our area were really in any measured way into grants. That began to develop during the '80s and has just continued. [Interview #4, card #16 of 175]

Dr. Wilson's priorities, too, have shifted over the years. While his primary focus may have been on obtaining external funds for research, today, his focus is on teaching and the service he provides to the department by taking on a large teaching load. This shift in priorities seems to have come from an experience of an automobile wreck, the injuries he sustained, and his subsequent recovery:

> At one time I had in one year six PhDs and four master's students. Keeps you very busy. When I got out of this, I was in a wreck that laid me up and I was pretty well out.

I didn't teach for a year. Then I came back. I was still not moving and I just got my ankle fused, it's been two years ago this month, and I'm back on my feet again. So I had a very slow period here but going into that I had grants, I had two postdocs, PhD and master's students. I got back on my feet literally and my grants had run out. The four proposals I had out were not funded and the postdoc periods had run out. I'd finished the master's and PhD and I was coming up on 60 years old and I said "do I want to try to start all this back up again?" And things weren't starting, I got much more involved, I've been president of my international professional society, picked up some more teaching in the department, so much more on service roles than other things. I've been doing research, and I've had little, but I'm not going back on the treadmill. That's when I told the department back about two department heads, back about 2000, I said this is where I'm going to go. If it doesn't fit, let me know, I'll give you the position back and move on. So I've tried to give value back to the department in what I'm doing and I don't think there is anybody who's unhappy that I'm holding a position down.

Dr. Wilson's teaching load is comparatively heavy. For example, he was responsible for five different classes and groups of students in Fall 2006, and he uses the course management system (CMS) available at University A, Blackboard Vista, to help him manage the course load. His teaching philosophy and views on technology used for teaching are provided below:

I try to have justice in my classes tempered with mercy and I offer grace where needed. So, yep, you've got to have rules, there has to be justice but rules can also be administered, depending on the case, with mercy. And occasionally you can assist students and push them over where they didn't think they could make it. So, some don't need it, few do, so that's my teaching philosophy. … But if technology gets in the way of that, it's a hindrance. If it facilitates, it's there but it also sets the context for knowledge. [Interview #4, cards #171-172 of 175]

More of Dr. Wilson's story will be shared later in *The Findings*.

University A and University B in the 1960's

Here, I will pause from the participant introductions and add relevant information regarding the research sites during the 1960's, the period when Dr. Wilson professionally became associated with University A.

According to the information available at the website of the parent system of both universities, University A opened its doors in the 1870s as a land-grant institution. Until 1963, it was a segregated institution accepting only white male students (Paddon, 2007). However, in 1963 University A became integrated as blacks and women were admitted, although apparently with much reluctance.

Another change swept through University A in 1963: the designation of College in its name became *University* (Fernandez, 1988). Nationally in the 1960s, universities across the US were embroiled in student protests against the Vietnam War. Even so, the students at University A evidently did not engage in such demonstrations because the university president of that era forbade such activities (Fernandez, 1988).

The 1960s was still three decades before University B would be officially formed. The dental school that would become one of its health professions schools, however, was in existence in another city since 1905.

Carl Andrews, 1976

Carl Andrews is originally from the Midwest, received his undergraduate degree from one major public research university there, and his graduate degrees from another major public research university in the same state. He arrived at University A in 1976, as an assistant professor, his first tenure-track faculty appointment. Today, Dr. Andrews is a tenured full professor.

Teaching both undergraduate and graduate statistics courses, Dr. Andrews belongs to a department which offers a master's program in statistics over the distance, completely online. One unique characteristic of Dr. Andrews' department is the commitment from the leadership on the infrastructural support for conducting distance education, removing many of the first-order barriers (Ertmer, 1999, 2005):

> You know our department is ... well it goes from the department head who's pushing this opportunity for us. We have a full professor who's also the associate dean for distance, I don't know, it's education or something like that. That associate dean, he's the one in charge of the graduate students, but he hired a full time person, who handles all the technical details. She's not a statistician but she's really great as far as making sure that the pen works, making sure the recording's okay and so I think that we're really lucky in our department. [Interview #8, card #17 of 74]

Furthermore, graduate students in the program serve as teaching assistants, provide technical assistance to the faculty who teach using educational technology, are available in the classroom when faculty are teaching, and perform all the necessary technical work before and after the class meetings. Thus, both junior and senior faculty appear to participate in teaching using educational technology. I asked Dr. Andrews if he would be teaching using educational technology without the support he currently receives. His answer was "probably not" [Interview #8, card #16 of 74]. More will be discussed later on this point when the research questions are addressed.

Peter Jones, 1977

Peter Jones is originally from the northern part of the US, "a beautiful, beautiful, country" [Interview #6, card #11 of 90]. He received an undergraduate degree in engineering, from his home state, and went south for his graduate degrees in statistics. Dr. Jones arrived at University A in 1977, after having taught one year each at two different universities. Today, he is a tenured full professor as well as an administrator. Dr. Jones too recalled the many changes that have occurred at University A and the town in which it resides:

> Oh, unbelievable changes. In the size, the attitude, the environment of this university plus the size and gains of sort of the outside interest in the town. The town was so small, the college town, when we came here in the '70s. It's unbelievably different. [Interview #6, card #14 of 90]

Furthermore, he shared his thoughts in the change in the political climate and cultural environment of the university:

> Amazing improvement since when I started. Absolutely. ... I won't get deep into politics but I'm a pretty liberal minded sort of person and it was very, very conservative when we first got here. Two, I think the ethnic diversity increased considerably. Still, it's nowhere near where it should be but I love that. Just the differences and cultures .... [Interview #6, card #84 of 90]

Dr. Jones teaches two graduate courses on statistical methods using educational technology. He reiterated the importance of the infrastructural support for teaching using educational technology available to him and other faculty members in his department:

> Well I think what really scares off a lot of faculty members is that they'd have to learn all the technology because we're busy to begin with, especially our department which is very, very research-oriented. So to get anybody other than a couple of us older people to do this, and I don't do much research anymore because of my administrative duties, to get any of the real research faculty to do it, they would never have done it without all the support. [Interview #6, card #26 of 90]

This point will be addressed further in *The Findings*, along with other emerged themes and subthemes.

Michael Johnston, 1977

Michael Johnston also arrived at University A in 1977. Originally from the Midwest, Dr. Johnston received his undergraduate degree from a large public research university in the Midwest and his graduate degrees from another large public research university, also in the Midwest. After a year of a postdoctoral experience, he started his first tenure-track position at University A in 1977. He has been a tenured full professor since 1990.

Dr. Johnston's use of educational technology for teaching includes a digital image library of vascular plants and associated web-based test drills. His foray into teaching using educational technology occurred as a byproduct of a locally funded interdisciplinary research grant that subsequently led to funding by the state's higher education coordinating board and then to funding by the National Science Foundation. However, among the 10 faculty members who participated in my study, Dr. Johnston appeared to be one of the most adversely affected by academic capitalism: his field, systematic botany, is evidently fading away:

> This money mill thing, in biology, it's kind of a complicated story. But molecular biology basically has revolutionized the discipline and the federal government, the funding through the federal government, has really hunkered down on molecular biology. And botany is a non-molecular, for the most part, discipline. It deals with whole organisms you know. So it has suffered from that point of view. And those institutions that focus on getting money ... now old botanical gardens, Harvard, Duke, Berkeley, quality educational institutions that still have strong programs in botany, although with the exception of Wisconsin and a few others, they don't call it botany. The term botany and zoology, these are archaic terms. To be politically correct you have to call them something else. [Interview #7, cards #92-93 of 110]

Consequently, Dr. Johnston has not been mentoring graduate students, neither master's nor doctoral:

> And I've refused to take students since 2000 and my administrators have not been happy with me for that refusal .... I hate to digress but our botany program just kind of disappeared. I'm kind of like the last surviving botanist, myself and my colleague. I just feel like I can't bring a

student in and actually prepare them as a botanist if there are no courses to take. [Interview #7, card #84]

I will return to Dr. Johnston's story later when the research questions are addressed in *The Findings*.

University B in 1977

Although two decades will pass before University B is officially formed, another future component, the medical school, opened its doors in 1977.

Erica Baker, 1985

Erica Baker is originally from the Pacific Coast. She received her undergraduate degree in psychology, through which she was able to design an interdisciplinary degree plan that focused on biology, psychology, and anthropology. Dr. Baker was motivated to pursue science as a result of doing undergraduate research in Europe:

> I spent some time off in Europe doing undergraduate research, what would you say, supplementary kind of an experience, where I actually worked with a person who won a Nobel Prize later. So all of that was part of what motivated me as a woman to choose to go into science. [Interview #2, cards #20-21 of 152]

She did her doctoral work in ecology and behavioral biology in the North and postdoctoral work in the South. Dr. Baker arrived at University A in 1985 as an assistant professor, her first tenure-track position, as the first woman to be hired by her department. She is a tenured associate professor today and teaches in areas related to animal behavior.

Some of the courses Dr. Baker teaches are fully online and uses University A's course management system, Blackboard Vista. She designs her courses around three elements: "comprehension, application, and synthesis of information" [Interview #2, card #29 of 152]. Dr. Baker echoed the adverse aspect of academic capitalism noted by Dr. Johnston, the aspect related to the phenomenon favoring certain fields over others:

> Well the thing with zoology is that it's going cellular, molecular because that's where the money is. And so we actually have accepted, organized more biologists whom they got rid of and pushed over into our department. [Interview #2, card #138 of 152]

And this push of non-cellular biologists to Dr. Baker's department seems to be occurring because her department focuses on the whole animal rather than on the cellular level, a focus preferred by Dr. Baker:

> And that's a personal thing, too because as a student, I wanted to learn with my own eyes, and ears, and nose. I wanted to use binoculars and not microscopes. And that's a bias. And I find that I connect with students who also have that shared bias. [Interview #2, card #140 of 152]

Dr. Baker's story, too, will be provided more in detail when the research questions are addressed in *The Findings*.

Sheryl Caldwell, 1995

Sheryl Caldwell is originally from the South Central US and attended schools in the same region to obtain her undergraduate, master's, and doctoral degrees. She arrived at University A in 1995 as an assistant professor, her first tenure-track position, while still completing her postdoctoral duties from another institution. Today, she is a tenured associate professor.

As a community ecologist, Dr. Caldwell travels across North America for data collection and teaches courses in animal ecology and fisheries management. She uses the Web to post her course materials, to aid her in course management, and to communicate with her students. Initially, she developed the web pages herself and used a website outside of a course management system (e.g.,. Blackboard Vista). Today, she uses Blackboard Vista (also referred to as WebCT, an older name for Blackboard Vista):

> My main mode is probably the WebCT. That's probably the most obvious one. But in the past, I've used websites that I simply made out of Microsoft files. This was probably about

five or six years ago. I was just converting all my documents into HTML files to upload to a website so students could have access to things like my syllabus, schedules, and documents. The last two years was the first time I actually used WebCT, not only as a way to provide documents but also to organize things like grades and to communicate with the students. [Interview #3, cards #16-17 of 165]

Although her position at University A is her first faculty appointment, Dr. Caldwell previously has held other non-faculty positions. Her motivation to pursue academia included her love of learning:

> ... probably one of the main reasons I actually came back and got my PhD and wanted to work at a university was I love learning. I am definitely a lifelong learner .... I had 15 years between each of my degrees, just about, and so each time I came back was because I was really attracted to learning. I was really attracted to research as a way to learn. [Interview #3, cards #150 of 165]

Another motivation for pursuing academia included her interest in conducting research and teaching:

> I enjoyed being a researcher 10-15 years. I was basically a researcher but a technologist when I worked in a hospital lab, but I enjoyed trying to figure out what was wrong with a patient, helping the doctor make a diagnosis and make that person well. Then after awhile I became just a technician running a machine and I wasn't doing as much of the investigative component of that on my own so that's when I went back to school the first time. The reason I went back to school for my PhD — I had been through 10 years, 15 years of research and I said "You know, I want to write my own research grants and I want to do my own things." I always had a focus on what went on in a seminar or a classroom between teachers and their students and between researchers and their students. To me, that was always attractive. [Interview #3, cards #152-153 of 165]

And, as you will see later in *The Findings*, Dr. Caldwell echoes a common theme found among the study participants—that the professoriate is a dream job, albeit a difficult one:

> Because I've had other jobs. I've had other jobs where I was totally in research, totally worked in the lab, and didn't have that educational component, and I think that really truly this is my dream job, although it's not easy. [Interview #3, card #159 of 165]

Theresa Wells, 1999

Theresa Wells was a military brat who "lived everywhere," although she was born in the region of the South Central US [Interview #5, card #2 of 158]. She fondly recalled her experiences of living in Japan. As a military brat myself, we shared our notes about living in the Far East during a similar period.

Dr. Wells received her undergraduate degree at University A and worked in non-faculty positions in another region of the US. She arrived at University B as an assistant professor, her first tenure-track position: (Reminder: University A and University B are located in the same city and belong to the same university system.)

> I went to college at this institution as an undergraduate and then went off and worked for awhile and ended up by backdoor means, ended up in epidemiology and for a health department in the East Coast. [Interview #5, card #2 of 158]

Her career path as a public health epidemiologist was a departure from her undergraduate degree, fishery science. However, she loved the new field, received her graduate degrees in the discipline, and returned to the south central region to work for a state public health department: "And I loved it so I went and got a master's and a doctorate and then came back to this state and worked for the health department" [Interview #5, card #2 of 158].

Because both University A and University B are located in the same city, she chuckled about returning to the city where she had received her undergraduate degree. Also, like Dr. Jones, she noted how the city has changed over the years, although from the perspective of someone who previously experienced the city as an undergraduate student:

> When I left here as an undergraduate, I said "that's it, Lord, did my time, I am so out of here" and to be back here, it's just funny. … When we moved back here, I was just astonished how 20 years later it is completely different. The wealth of the students just floors me. … We were doing well if one of us among our group of friends had a car. And to see BMWs and really nice vehicles and very luxurious apartment complexes, the culture is very, very different. … I think the student body was a lot smaller so you were more likely to know a good chunk of people. It really has exploded. It's not a bad thing, it's just a lot different than my experience. And this area wasn't a town. It really didn't exist. A few blocks off of campus, a town existed, and the older houses did. The mall and all of that were just fields so anything kind of past about where the mall is now was maybe a few scattered houses. So this area has become an actual town on its own and with very dramatic changes. Dramatic changes in that it's interesting to be here as faculty to see it from the other side because it's very different from what I imagined it was when I was here as a student. [Interview #5, cards #9-12 of 158]

The public health school of University B, to which Dr. Wells belongs, offers a master's degree to both residential and distance students. Therefore, Dr. Wells uses Blackboard Vista to teach a course that strictly meets online, for the distance cohorts, and to supplement a course that meets face-to-face, for the residential students.

Today, Dr. Wells is a tenured associate professor. More will be shared about Dr. Wells' experiences in *The Findings*.

University B in 1999

University B was officially formed in 1999 as a health professions university. Its components in 1999 included the schools
of dentistry, medicine, and public health.

Larry Smith, 2000

Larry Smith is originally from the Southeast US. Having completed his bachelor's and master's degrees at a major research
university in the Southeast, he completed his doctoral degree
at a major research university in the Midwest. Dr. Smith arrived
at University A in 2000 as an assistant professor, his first faculty appointment. Prior to his faculty appointment, he worked in
various capacities that included educational outreach. Today,
he is a tenured full professor in education.

Dr. Smith uses a variety of educational technologies to suit
the different teaching and learning needs. After listing the different technologies he incorporates into his teaching, he stated:

> … There are different purposes for using the technologies.
> So what I'm trying to do to design my course around is an
> expanded version of Moore's transactional distance the-
> ory. I try to find ways to maximize learner-learner inter-
> actions, learner to technology, learner to instructor, and
> learner to content, so I really use a variety of educational
> technologies. [Interview #1, card #8 of 159]

Dr. Smith's department offers both a master's and a doctoral
degree that are offered over the distance. He shared his department's views on the terminology *distance education*:

> We try not to use the word distance education anymore. …
> It's kind of a passé term. I know that in Europe and around
> the rest of the world e-learning kind of is still the pretty
> hot terminology but those of us at least in this department
> we thought about it a lot and we try to use technology-
> assisted learning because the research is so overwhelming
> that it doesn't matter. In terms of learning outcomes it
> doesn't matter if you're face-to-face or you're at a distance,
> or whether you're synchronous or asynchronous. The

learning outcomes, at least as we measure them in terms of grades and projects and stuff, there really isn't any difference. So because of that we try to move away and to say technology-assisted learning. And that's much broader. It just says how we teach. We tend to be very technology-rich in our teaching. [Interview #3, cards #16-18 of 159]

James Williams, 2000

James Williams, a "faculty brat" [Interview #10, card #4 of 110], was born in the Midwest US and lived in the Northeast and Midwest as his father's academic career took his family from one region to another. He attended a prestigious private institution in the Northeast for his undergraduate degree and returned to the Midwest for his graduate degrees, to the same university where his father is a faculty member:

> I went back to the university where I essentially grew up, despite my best attempts not to, for graduate school. I wanted to go somewhere else but the person that I really needed to work for was there. I was not so happy about going back home, I wanted to go to California or someplace. [Interview #10, card #6 of 110]

Dr. Williams arrived at University A in 2000 as an assistant professor in physics, his first faculty appointment, after completing a postdoctoral position at a federal national laboratory for conducting basic research in particle physics. Although this position is his first academic appointment, he worked during his graduate years as a teaching assistant and enjoyed the experience. And, his mentors identified him early on as an ideal candidate for the professoriate:

> ... I was identified early as being somebody who was going to be good at this. When I walked into the door, they pegged me. ... We had a class we had to take for TA training. I walked in the door and they knew right away. I would always be picked to do the demonstrations of how to teach. [Interview #10, card #10 of 110]

Dr. Williams uses a variety of educational technologies including Microsoft PowerPoint, to generate lecture slides, and the assessment feature in Blackboard Vista (or WebCT, as he refers to it below):

> I have used a number of tools. The one I use the most is PowerPoint overhead slides with all the cool tools in PowerPoint, you know, the videos, stuff flying in, things moving, I use that in every lecture. ... I use WebCT extensively as a homework and quiz delivery and collection system, thousands and thousands of quizzes per semester, well, hundreds of thousands of quizzes administered per semester. Very high statistics. [Interview #10, card #13 of 110]

Dr. Williams uses the Blackboard/WebCT quiz delivery feature to provide students with numerous drill and practice opportunities to help them learn to solve physics calculations.

Dr. Williams is a tenured associate professor today and more will be said about his experiences in *The Findings*.

Lindsay Reeves

Lindsay Reeves is originally from the Pacific Northwest. She received her undergraduate degree in nursing and a professional degree in law, both from the Pacific Northwest region. She practiced health and medical law in the Pacific Northwest first and in the Northeast next. She began her doctoral degree in public health in the Northeast and completed it after she arrived at University B as an assistant professor in public health. That was in 2001; today, Dr. Reeves is a tenured associate professor.

Although her current position at University B is her first tenure-track faculty appointment, because of her background, she was involved in teaching early on, even as a doctoral student:

> I taught immediately upon entering the PhD program. They needed someone to teach health law and since that was my specialty they put me in that mode and I continued to teach health law and risk management for health managers and also some of the courses in medical outcomes. [Interview #9, card #7 of 102]

Dr. Reeves uses a variety of educational technologies that includes Microsoft PowerPoint slides, videos, and websites. Because she teaches both residential students and distance cohorts enrolled in the school's master's program in public health, she also relies on the videoconferencing technology:

> In a classroom that's equipped to televise to distant sites, I have both a live classroom in the immediate classroom and in most years I've had a distance site linked out ... at the same time. [Interview #9, card #11 of 102]

Some courses she teaches are delivered mostly online:

> I've put my human resource management class online and made it available to students as a web-based course. We meet the first night live and during that time I show how to access all the important sites and move from page to page so that they don't have to find it on their own. [Interview #9, card #15 of 102]

Dr. Reeves' experiences, too, will be revisited in *The Findings*.

Summary of the Participants and the Research Sites

This section introduced the attributes of the 10 study participants: their biographical data such as the regions where they were raised and attended schools; professional data such as when they began their tenure track positions; and experiential views such as their motivation to pursue the professoriate, thoughts on infrastructural support for teaching using educational technology, and perspectives on the adverse effects of academic capitalism.

This section also introduced a few of the major changes that occurred at the research sites beginning from the 1960s, the decade when the study participant with the longest tenure arrived at University A. For University A, its transformation in 1963 from a white male only college to that of an integrated university—by race and gender—seems to be noteworthy. For University B, its birth in 1999 that brought together the different health professions components under one university appears to be significant.

Now, I will address the findings, delivered via the three research questions. This section follows below.

The Findings

The purpose of this interpretive critical inquiry was three-fold: (a) to understand the experiences of faculty at public research universities who teach using educational technology and their perceptions of how the demands of two apparently conflicting requirements of teaching using educational technology and obtaining externally funded research grants affect their job satisfaction as professors; (b) based on the findings, to offer suggestions and recommendations for organizational change that will serve to alleviate the conflicts faculty may experience; and (c) to identify the implications for human resource development (HRD) in public research universities in terms of addressing academic capitalism and teaching using educational technology.

The three research questions that guided the study were: (a) What is the experience of faculty members who teach using educational technology at a public research university? (b) How is the experience affecting them as more demands are placed on faculty to obtain external research funds? and (c) How is the experience affecting their job satisfaction? In this section, each research question will be addressed using the themes and subthemes that emerged from the interview data; an overview of the findings is provided below.

Research Question 1.
What is the experience of faculty members who teach using educational technology at a public research university?

The Association for Educational Communications and Technology (AECT), a professional organization for the field of educational technology, defines educational technology as "the study and ethical practice of facilitating learning and improving performance by creating, using, and managing appropriate technological processes and resources" (Januszewski, 2006, p. 10). Distance education, or distance learning, is "a form of education in which some means, electronic or otherwise, is used to connect people with instructors and/or resources that can help them acquire knowledge and skills" (Roblyer, 2006, p. G-3). In this study, distance education is viewed as a form of learning that makes use of educational technology.

Educational technology can be a wide range of tools that facilitate teaching and learning. The study participants' use of educational technology supported this perspective.

The following page provides the descriptions of the various educational technology products and components referred to by the participants. Thus, the study participants appear to make use of a variety of educational technologies in their teaching that range in complexity from simple technology, such as the whiteboard, to something more complex, such as a computer expert system, with different pedagogical goals or motivation for teaching using educational technology.

Three common subthemes emerged related to this research question of understanding the faculty experience in teaching using educational technology. The three subthemes were: (a) benefits, rationale, or motivation, (b) barriers, and (c) institutional/departmental support. They are described below.

Benefits, Rationale, or Motivation

The experience of teaching using educational technology appeared to be personally rewarding for the participants. Some participants stated they loved the experience. Here is Dr. Well's response: "Now, I love the web thing. Me personally, it suits me to a T. It really suits me" [Interview #5, card #31 of 158]. Dr. Jones shared a similar response: "I love it. Absolutely" [Interview #6, card #32 of 90].

A4
A7

Dr. Baker also stated that she loves the experience. She elaborated why:

> I actually love it. I've really enjoyed the distance ed class and the distance ed section of my mixed mode class, which is an undergrad class. And the reason is because I feel like I have better communication with the students in the chat

room. There's more one-on-one, there's more aha, and again those aha moments are the intangible moments that we never really measure. But for me as a teacher, it is my own gut measurement as to whether I'm doing a good job or not. [Interview #2, card #66 of 152]

B3   The reasons behind the personally rewarding experience seemed to vary but appeared to be because the participants realized one or more benefits as a result of teaching using educational technology. These benefits, in turn, seemed to serve as rationale or motivation. For some, the reason seemed to be related to the creativity in teaching using educational technology as shared by Dr. Johnston:

> Well, it's been interesting and exhilarating from an academic point of view. ... but from a teaching point of view I think the interest is in the development and the kind of creative manipulation of materials for a faculty member. The interest is not necessarily in the response you're going to get from either the administration or the student. [Interview #7, card #50 of 110]

A6   Dr. Reeves made a similar point:

> ... I'm really pleased with what I've been able to create, sort of an artistic pleasure. I look at that page and sometimes think "gee this is really neat." This sitting up there on the Web, this is my course. [Interview #9, card #92 of 102]

A6
A7   For Dr. Wells, creativity as well as learning something new were reasons for the personally rewarding experience in teaching using educational technology. In fact, the creativity and challenge of teaching in a new environment served to rejuvenate her interest in the course she had been teaching for years:

> ... the creativity and learning new technology. Academics are generally inquisitive people who are always sort of in a learning mode. That's what drew us into this the first place

so it's very refreshing to be challenged with teaching in a different environment. I was getting a little burned out. ... I was pretty much ready to say "I've had it, I've been doing this for six or seven years ... ." ... So this has rejuvenated my interest in teaching that course, by taking it into a whole different direction. [Interview #5, cards #117-118 of 158]

For other participants, the experience of teaching using educational technology provided positive outcomes because they were able to extend their efforts using technology, as in Dr. Wilson's case:

The backend—it's time saving. I was handling these five groups—I meet with the undergrad team once a week, I had the writing seminar class which has lots of papers to grade every week, I had the undergrad lab and writing every week, I had the undergrad lab I supervise, I had the 150 student lecture that I did last fall. Technology allowed me to do that and make it manageable. I had 270 students that I had contact with last fall in these 5 different classes and groups. So, yeah, technology is a way to extend my efforts .... [Interview #4, card #90 of 175]

A6
A7
    Another benefit from teaching using educational technology appeared to be pedagogical in that it could facilitate teaching and learning. For example, Dr. Smith mentioned how educational technology could enhance learning: "Yeah, it does enhance learning. Well, the research supports it and we certainly believe it, if done correctly" [Interview #1, card #30 of 159]. Dr. Baker shared how she was able to provide opportunities for students to take responsibility in their learning through the online chat tool:

But that actually is another benefit — that there are times when I turn the leadership of the chat over to one student and so there's a little bit of that leadership development that's actually beneficial because, again, they're taking responsibility for their learning. [Interview #2, card # 81 of 152]

Dr. Jones from the statistics department, whose lectures were recorded for access by local and distance students, saw technology as a way for students to pay attention to the content rather than on the act of taking notes:

> ... all we were asking them to be were stenographers. You know in stat a lot of it is formulas, even if I was doing examples, it takes a lot to write all the stuff down. And so now, we're able to let them listen. And really propose questions. ... Before they were writing so far back, like if you were doing a board, they were usually half a board behind you. [Interview #6, card #30 of 90]

B2   Still another benefit from teaching using educational technology appeared to be the ability to deliver learning to distance students, students who otherwise would not have had access to higher education. Here is Dr. Smith's perspective on the benefit of educational technology for serving distance education:

> At a distance, having grown up on a farm and worked for an extension, I think we get to reach people we otherwise would never reach. So for students who are truly at a distance, that's really good. [Interview #1, card #86 of 159]

A similar sentiment was shared by Dr. Caldwell: "For me, I'm predisposed to do it because I know we have a lot of students off campus who would like to be able to access courses. I didn't realize this" [Interview #3, card #51 of 165].

B2   For Dr. Wells, the option to deliver a course over the Web was beneficial both to her and her students:

> ... because it goes out to the distance cohorts. That was part of the rationale for me doing it. Because we have to catch the distance students and we have to teach at night. And I hate teaching at night. It's the worst time. They're tired. These are often students who work full time and are doing the program in the evening and they are just tired. They're burned out, I'm tired, and I figured that course

would be the best one to start with online because they could do it on their own time and at their own rate. [Interview #5, card #73 of 158]

Along the line of Dr. Wells' comments above, flexibility and convenience—both to the participants and students—afforded by educational technology was another common subtheme of benefits. Dr. Wilson spoke of the flexibility he gained by conducting online quizzes:

> Frustrations of using class time for quizzes, all the paper to deal with. With large classes you've got to get scans, the hassle of having the bubble sheets, get them over there [to the testing center to process the bubble sheets]. The amount of copies you had to run and then the ease of use of that [online quiz system]. You can build your stuff, you can change things, a student misses one, you can have the open closed dates, you can use selective availability. It has a lot of nice features which in a class with 150 students, those are really nice. It allows me to have some flexibility to deal with things. You can do the other way but it's just a lot easier. [Interview #4, card #65 of 175]

Dr. Johnston, too, shared his views on the flexibility provided by educational technology. His perspectives, though, were from the flexibility in content access and self-assessment provided to the students:

> I guess the third element involves material available for the student to access at anytime, which the technology provides that we didn't have before. And that involved in addition to taking the material that we present to the students also working out little test drills that they could do anytime that they wanted to, computer-based. [Interview #7, card #11 of 110]

B2
B3
C13
D2

The last common subtheme of benefits from teaching using educational technology was it can promote lifelong learning that facilitated the self-perceived need to keep up with the students. Here are Dr. Caldwell's thoughts: "Just learning new things. Actually, it keeps you up with the students. Well, I never like to feel like I'm behind on anything" [Interview #3, card #95 of 165]. Dr. Wells also stressed that she felt the need to keep up with the current generation of students who seems to possess a short attention span due to the media-rich environment with which they are accustomed:

> So there is something unsettling about using the technology. On the one hand, you're keeping up with, I think, how students receive information in their lives. They're very media oriented and they're very visual. The attention span issue is huge to me. I think you can see the effects of such a media-oriented youth. The kids that are coming through now started with computers. They've always had a lot of television, a lot of visuals, and a lot of graphics so if you just stand in front of them and talk, they don't know what to do with you. So I use the technology because I have to keep up with them. [Interview #5, card #18 of 158]

C13
D2

Overall, the participants appeared to be pleased with the outcomes of teaching using educational technology and stated various benefits that perhaps served as rationale or motivation to teach using educational technology. To apply the terms of first-order/second-order barriers, where first-order barriers are *extrinsic* obstacles that occur external to the teacher, such as an inadequate infrastructure or technical support, and second-order barriers are *intrinsic* obstacles that occur as a result of an innate characteristic such as the teacher's belief system (Ertmer, 1999, 2005), the rationale or motivation too can be described as either first-order or second-order. Most rationale or motivation appeared to be second-order, that is, they were intrinsic to the participants: personal satisfaction from creativity and challenge in teaching using educational technology, belief that it enhances teaching and learning, and a vehicle for faculty's lifelong learning. First-order rationale or motivation included a way to extend faculty efforts, reach distance students, and provide flexibility and convenience to local and distance students.

However, the journey to realizing the positive end results did not appear to be a smooth road. They spoke of many barriers that challenged them. The next section addresses the barriers that emerged as another common subtheme.

Barriers

The participants shared four categories of barriers they experienced: (a) time constraints, (b) steep learning curves, (c) technical problems, and (d) pedagogical challenges. These barriers are discussed below.

J2
G5

Time constraints. This barrier was the most mentioned barrier among the study participants. For Dr. Smith, the barrier regarding time was twofold. One, spending time on educational technology was at the expense of focusing on activities that provided greater rewards to professors at research universities: "The barrier is that it takes time away from the other things" [Interview #1, card #71 of 159]. Two, teaching using educational technology consumes more time than teaching traditionally without technology: "And most of us who do it will say that it takes a lot more time to prepare and monitor and to run these courses at a distance than as a face-to-face" [Interview #1, card #21 of 159]. Dr. Baker echoed this time consuming characteristic of teaching using educational technology: "... it was so incredibly time consuming for me to try to learn all of that stuff on my own ..." [Interview #2, card #52 of 152]. She elaborated on this point:

> Sheer time of prepping the materials. Getting familiar with the programs and then that they're updated so you feel like the Red Queen, running, running, running always trying to learn a new tool and that's a barrier because my frustration level gets to the point where I feel like my time is being wasted on the tools rather than on the content and delivery. [Interview #2, card #72 of 152]

The time burden was also an issue for Dr. Wilson. However, he did note that time efficiencies were gained later.

Technology takes a lot of time. Instructor time. It's expensive. There are some payoffs in it once you get it done, it has some efficiencies. But the upfront cost and the learning threshold is a significant cost and keeps a lot of our faculty out of it. [Interview #4, card #86 of 175]

However, being members of a department that provided full technical support for teaching using educational technology, Dr. Jones did not experience any time constraints and Dr. Andrews experienced time constraints but not related to learning or operating the technology. Here is Dr. Jones' response when I asked him if he experienced any barriers or challenges:

"I would think just learning the technology, if you had to. Like I said we're in the ideal situation where the graduate students are doing all the work. I don't have to learn the technology" [Interview #6, card #33 of 90].

Dr. Andrews did experience time constraints but they were brought on by the increased student enrollment as a result of his department's participation in distance education: "It's more, having more students, it's more time evaluating their work, grading, and so forth. That increases the time burden" [Interview #8, card #28 of 74]. Dr. Wells too found this increase in workload to be true for her:

It's a lot more work to put together all those resources, to follow up on students, to read emails, to keep on top of it, as opposed to a course you go in and you teach three hours and you're done. [Interview #5, card #108 of 158]

To address the time constraints, Dr. Reeves dedicated her weekends to developing her web-based course materials:

… the first year I did it, it just took an enormous amount of time. And that amount of time I basically carved out my Saturdays and came in and videotaped while no one else was around. [Interview #9, card #17 of 102]

D5 Finally, Dr. Williams, too, shared his thoughts regarding the
D8 time-consuming nature of teaching using educational tech-
E1 nology. As shown below in an interview excerpt, the rich
E2 educational technology components textbook publishers read-
ily make available to professors did not seem to help either:

> Dr. Williams: So there are all these great textbooks that
> you can buy and they say here's our lectures and here are
> videos but if you could have used their stuff. You have to
> use their lectures but I don't want to use their lectures, I
> want to put their stuff into my lecture but they don't use
> PowerPoint, they use something else. And they say here
> are these really cool graphics and I'm going to bring in the
> graphics but they made graphics so that they work in Mic-
> rosoft Windows Explorer but I don't want to use, I don't
> want to stop my lecture and pull up Microsoft Explorer
> and then show a video and then go back to my PowerPoint.
> I want the thing to show up in my PowerPoint and I want to
> put arrows in to point at what I think is important. I want
> to start it and stop it and restart it and move it backwards
> and forwards and they're not many people who know how
> to do that and I've had to learn how to do that.
>
> Researcher: And that part is very time consuming.
>
> Dr. Williams: VERY time consuming. The investment
> to learn how to do that is ENORMOUS. [Interview #10,
> cards #52-53 of 110; capitalized words represent the
> emphases the participant made during the interview.]

Learning curves. This barrier referred to the steep learning curves
that accompanied using educational technology to teach. Perhaps this barrier is another perspective of the time constraint
barrier for the amount of time one needs to invest to overcome
a steep learning curve could be significant. Here is Dr. Wilson's
experience regarding the steep learning curve of a tool:

> Learning how to run the software. I've got to learn by next
> fall how to operate Vista 4, use it in peer groups and manage

groups and all of that. That's going to take quite a few hours of my time this summer. [Interview #4, card #87 of 175]

A10 *Technical problems.* Adding to the barriers of time constraints
A9   and steep learning curves were issues related to the instability, unpredictability, or unreliability of technology. Dr. Caldwell stated matter-of-factly that "... you've got to be prepared for the unknown. It's not a perfect world, especially if you're doing live classroom technology" [Interview #3, card #92 of 165]. Dr. Wells had similar experiences: "... and sometimes the technology just crashes. For example, just flat out WebCT goes down and just doesn't work" [Interview #5, card #114 of 158].

A10 Another perspective of the barrier related to technical problems
B3   is that the participants often were sought out by their students to help resolve technical glitches. Dr. Wells shared her thoughts on this point: "... or students don't understand their computers are older so they have connectivity problems and you spend a lot of time just troubleshooting their access to the course" [Interview #5, card #114 of 158]. Sometimes, the need for the participants to serve as technical support persons seemed to occur at the least opportune time, as shared by Dr. Reeves:

> At times there is a conflict. Especially at the beginning of a semester. If I happened to have something due on a research grant or a proposal that could go out and yet I'm responding to distressed students who seemed to can't get in or are having trouble because they've a dial-up modem and they suddenly realized they need a broadband. That has to take priority and I've got to push other things aside. [Interview #9, card #85 of 102]

B9   The issue of slower bandwidth was a recurring problem for a handful of Dr. Reeves' students because they were not able to view the videos she had incorporated into her web-based course materials. She devised a workaround solution: "so what we end up doing is making DVDs or CDs of the videos for them and send them out via mail" [Interview #9, card #57 of 102].

Pedagogical challenges. The participants also mentioned the pedagogical challenges they had to address in order to teach using educational technology. Some challenges pertained to the difficulty in converting learning activities that occurred in the face-to-face environment. Others pertained to communicating or connecting with the students. For example, Dr. Jones shared a potential constraint in conducting two activities for his distance students in the master's statistics program:

> But we require them to do a master's project so they get a writing experience. And that's going to be a little trickier doing at a distance because a lot of times with writing you really need a sort of a face-to-face discussion. And we'll see how that works out. That's one point. Two, we require them to have two semesters of consulting experience. So this help desk or consulting center that I run, I do a lot of hands-on with it too. ... Plus we have a weekly staff meeting where everybody who's enrolled gets together and talks about all the problems that are giving them difficulties. And how we will do that at a distance, provide the same consulting experience for these master's students, we haven't quite figured out how we're going to do that. [Interview #6, cards 76-77 of 90]

Dr. Wells shared her challenges in connecting with the students:

> And then you have the creating a classroom environment with people that you never see. So connecting with students is more challenging. When you're lecturing to them you can see when they're not getting it. But when you've set it up online you really have to work hard. I included a lot of a little self-study quizzes that did not cost them anything if they took them but I could see if it took them 10 attempts to get a 100%. Or, I'll do surveys in between. There's a lot more work than just if I'm lecturing in front of them. I can stop and ask questions and know right away this is not

going where I thought it was going. So that can be a little frustrating. [Interview #5, card 115 of 158]

J1   Sometimes, pedagogical concerns surfaced as a result of student responses to learning using educational technology, such as in Dr. Reeves' case, whose students enrolled in a web-based course compared the online experience with that of a face-to-face experience:

> So I don't know how they respond to my videos but I think overall the expressions and opinions I've gotten is that "gee, having taken your health law course, I really miss the discussions about those interesting issues and I wish we could have that in a web-based course." [Interview #9, card #25 of 102]

J3a   In summary, the common barriers shared by the participants
H7b   were time constraints, steep learning curves, technical problems, and various pedagogical challenges. Furthermore, these barriers appeared to be interrelated in that attending to the steep learning curves and technical problems exacerbated the time constraint burden. This time constraint burden, however, appeared to be minimized when a participant's department, such as Dr. Jones', provided human resources (Warschauer, 2002) for addressing technical issues as part of its infrastructure for teaching using educational technology. Also, although the participants typically spoke about the steep curve in learning a new educational technology product, the pedagogical challenges they shared signaled another learning curve: learning the pedagogy of teaching using educational technology.

J3a   Thus, the issue of the learning curves seemed to denote two needs—a need to become facile in using the tools and a need to develop an expertise in the pedagogy of teaching using the tools. These needs could be addressed through human resource development (HRD), some of which were provided at University A as faculty development workshops. The next section discusses the final subtheme related to this research question—the institutional and/or departmental support.

Institutional/Departmental Support

The institutional support for educational technology at University A included an office (OET) that provided physical resources (e.g., hardware, software) and human resources (e.g., training and technical support) (Warschauer, 2002) for teaching using educational technology. These resources were also available to University B. The physical resources included Blackboard Vista (WebCT) and other software and equipment for faculty use. Human resources included a range of faculty development workshops on products such as Blackboard Vista and TechSmith Camtasia as well as workshops on various how-to topics such as how to incorporate video into web pages, how to select a media player, and how to configure the browser to support multimedia applications. The participants who have used the services of that department rated it favorably as exemplified by this statement by Dr. Baker: "They were wonderful in helping me with the steep learning curve as far as getting into the first levels of WebCT and as far as all of the upgrades that have come along with WebCT" [Interview #2, card #74 of 152].

B7   However, Dr. Smith thought University A's institutional support for carrying out distance education was lacking: "The university has no concerted effort to do distance education. There is no centralized, purposeful way that the university wants to do distance education" [Interview #1, card #82 of 159]. When I pointed out that there might be an office for distance education at University A, he was surprised. He searched for the office at the university's website during our interview and indeed found it. He read the description of the office available at the website but seemed to think that the description was less than sincere. Here is an excerpt of our conversation:

Dr. Smith: I didn't even know this existed. Isn't it interesting?

Researcher: Would you still feel that it's more of a lip service?

Dr. Smith: Sure! What are they doing for me? Right? What are they doing for me? Tell me one thing they are doing for me. Nothing.

[Interview #1, cards #83-84 of 159].

B8   Even though Dr. Smith found University A's office of distance education suspect, he too was happy with the services provided by the other office, OET.

The one group of people would be WebCT [referring to the department that supports Blackboard Vista] .... No, we need them. We absolutely need them. They actually work with faculty members. [Interview #1, card #85 of 159]

Some participants received support at the college level and found this support valuable. Dr. Baker shared her experience of using her college's support for instructional design:

Like this semester, we're going through a process of streamlining the materials so I needed the outside help, I needed the professional help, the services from the distance education office in my college. And so they are going through and basically looking at my materials. One of the complaints I've had from the students was that there was too much and that it needed to be streamlined. And so they're going through and looking at it in terms of comparison with other materials, other courses, streamlining it, making sure that there's kind of a one-step, 1, 2, 3, 4 this is how you get started .... [Interview #2, card #5 of 152]

B8   Dr. Caldwell also found the design support available at the same college helpful:

In fact, having had someone to help, quote, unquote, and I love her to death, help me to design a web course – she got it up and going and she makes it happen [Interview #3, card #88 of 165].

B9   Sometimes, the support seemed to be in knowledge sharing that also appeared to serve as social resource (Warschauer, 2002), such as in Dr. Wells' case:

The assistant dean here is very into the technology for distance learning so he's a great resource. Yeah, he's really good. He tends to test out a bunch of new software and he'll come by and give me the links and say "okay, go try this, go try this." [Interview #5, card #95 of 158]

B15   One noteworthy situation was from Dr. Jones' and Dr. Andrews' department, the one that provides a complete support for teaching using educational technology through assistance from graduate students, full-time staff, and associate dean for distance education. In fact, the support provided seemed to represent three of the four necessary resources in Warschauer's (2002) technology for social inclusion: physical (hardware and software), human (technical support), and social (supportive departmental culture). An impetus behind the full support appears to be administrators very knowledgeable about delivering distance education:

Our current department head started in March of 2005. He came to us from a university in Australia and had been teaching distance learning courses through the MBA program there. So he had a vast experience in doing this. Number one. And number two, one of our faculty members has had a very strong interest in distance learning for a number of years. And matter of fact I think most people on this campus would say he knows more about the technology of distance learning than anybody else by far. [Interview #6, cards #7 of 90].

B 19   Other driving forces appeared to be a perceived demand for distance education in statistics and the department's commitment to teaching. Dr. Andrews shared his thoughts on the demand for a distance-based master's program in statistics:

> Big demand from industry, two sources: Industry, many people who go to the industry—they either have a math degree or a computer science degree. There's not enough statisticians working in this industry, or government, or even the medical research facilities that there's a big demand for someone who can analyze the data. So these people, by being the most quantitative people generally in the group, they end up with the job. They can run the computer programs. And these people would like to learn much more about statistics because they can do a better analysis. They don't want to give up their jobs, though, and they may live in California, or Japan, or China, or any place and want to get a master's degree. So that was the demand. That was one. The second demand, potentially, is for high school math teachers who are teaching AP stat. Many of them are again mathematics teachers, very little training in statistics, but they're sort of given the job because no one else is qualified to do it but really would like to understand a much greater depth of what they're teaching to the AP students. So that's another market that we're hoping that we can capture. [Interview #6, cards #5-6 of 90]

Distance education appears to be an effect of academic capitalism and this point will be discussed further under *Research Question 2*.

B 15   I asked Dr. Jones what prompted his department to be com-
C 1   mitted to teaching since his department, ranked in the top 15 nationally and "pushing towards top 10" [Interview #6, card #85 of 90] is also "very very strong research-orientated" [card #26 of 90]. The following excerpt is our resulting conversation:

Researcher: So what motivates your department to really spend a lot of effort on teaching, do you think?

Dr. Jones: We just have a commitment to good teaching. We always have. One demonstration of that is the enormous number of our faculty members who have won university and college level teaching awards. There has always been a commitment to teaching from the top down. So when new faculty members come in, new assistant profs, we've hired a lot of new assistant profs because we're part of our previous president's growth program, they're told we expect high quality teaching. What we do is their teaching load is only two courses for the first two years of their appointment.

Researcher: Entire year?

Dr. Jones: Yeah, usually one a semester. But occasionally we'll give them two in a semester and actually give them another semester off. And for the first two years, it's the only course. There's no new development. They only have to develop one course. And generally it's a course that we've had already very much developed so there are tons of material for them. So their only responsibility, basically, is to deliver that product to the students so they don't have to spend a lot of time preparing notes, exercises, they have to of course prepare the exams new. But we give them a lot of support. We emphasize the teaching part. Because we all know if you want to stay at this place you've got to pump out research and get grant money. So we want high quality teaching while they're doing this other stuff. So luckily, we're big enough and have good people in here for the teaching side.

C5
C6   Other examples of the full support for teaching using educational technology available at the department included the human resources: besides the associate dean for distance education and full-time staff, the department also hires graduate assistants who provide support:

Matter of fact, the way we do it is the student, new incoming student, takes this course because it is taken by all first year students, whether master's or PhD. What we do then is to train these students a couple weeks before the semester starts. Since they actually are taking my class, if I have a problem with a technology during the lecture, and it doesn't happen very often, every once in a while something goes wrong, they're right there to fix it. [Interview #6, card#23 of 90]

Thus, a benefit of the graduate student support was that the technology seemed to be transparent to the participants:

... the nice thing is our department has graduate students so that I just have to walk into the classroom and teach and they'll come in and have everything set up. And then at the end of the class they will take care of the Camtasia recording and the Centra recording. [Interview #8, card #14 of 74]

Furthermore, the support seemed to have allowed the participants to focus on their *teaching* rather than on the technology: "So my responsibility is the content of the course and the actual teaching" [Interview #8, card #15 of 74]. In addition, a distinguished professor also teaches a distance course:

... matter of fact, he teaches one of the DL courses. He's like one of the top ten statisticians in the whole world and yet he teaches a course and students just love it. He only teaches like every other year because of his research demands but when he does teach it, I can put it into an auditorium of 200 probably. [Interview #6, card #53 of 90]

C14
E8
A contrasting case appeared to be Drs. Wells and Reeves' college. Both Drs. Wells and Reeves teach using educational technology to address their college's mission of providing public health education to the remote and underserved regions of the state. Therefore they teach using the videoconferencing technology as well as over the Web.

Besides attending to the mission, another reason the faculty at the college may teach using educational technology seemed to be to respond to a movement in their field to offer the master of public health (MPH) degree over the Web: "We have an MPH and there are a variety of universities that now offer completely online MPHs" [Interview #5, card #32 of 158]. Thus, the administrators appeared to have placed an expectation on the faculty to convert the core courses into an online format: "So the first step towards an online degree was to get all the core courses online. … I think they want within two years to have all of them, all the core courses, online" [Interview #5, cards #64-65 of 158]. This apparent response to a movement in their field also seems to be an effect of academic capitalism: the use of distance education as a means to address the perception of a demand. This point will be discussed further in *Research Question 2*.

D5
C9
G2b
H4
H7b(2)

The excerpt below seems to illustrate a case of a push to embrace distance education by administrators inexperienced in carrying out distance education:

> Dr. Wells: But they did that without … this university and many of the colleges give an incentive to faculty like a payment of $3000—$5000 to develop an online course out of their onsite course. There was no incentive at all here. There was nothing. There were no resources, there was no salary incentive and the only incentive for me to do this was I didn't want to teach at night and I was curious about this technology. So not surprisingly other faculty haven't really jumped on. Unless they're motivated themselves, it's a lot of work to expect of people. … So there is no way they are going to meet the 2-year timeline and have it all by basically the end of next year …. This school unfortunately made this decision without any practical resources so now they're sort of playing catch-up. And we realize that it's not as simple … I think there were administrators who thought … one thing they thought was well you can just record all your onsite ones and just put them on the Web. And so I've gone

back to multiple meetings and said "that's the poorest use of both resources." That's like the worst you could do to students. Because it's like videoconferencing but even worse because you have no interactions and plus you usually have poor quality of the recording. And having gotten into the literature of distance delivery, I've learned that's just a horrible, horrible way to try to teach. So I've gone back to them and said "there's a quality issue and I'm going to be embarrassed for us as a school if that's the default, if people just record their lecture and throw it up. It's a different environment and faculty need to understand that. They're going to need some training and they're going to need to do some re-thinking of their materials because a voice-over Power-Point is not the way to go every single time. And for some it may get worse, but mostly it's not the environment where they're going to learn. You're going to drive students nuts doing that." So they've at least stopped saying ...

Researcher: Oh, have they?

Dr. Wells: Yeah, yeah, it's taken some education because they were originally thinking "well, we could grow all these students because we can just give them an online class." No, it doesn't work that way. It's not automated so that you can put 100 students on. I think they had a vision that it was a thing, a product, that you just put out there and it sort of goes along by itself and takes care of itself. No, it's still class requiring faculty time, you can't just have a bunch more distance cohorts and expect one person to now have a class of 100. First of all, you need to cap it. I don't know how you do more than 20 meaningfully. Probably 15's better at a graduate level. So you can't have a 60-person class. You'd be doing nothing but reading emails all day. So I think I've gotten them backed up to realizing there are a lot of limitations and it's not a magic answer to growth in the school. And they're going to have to convince faculty that it's worth their time, especially tenured faculty. Why would they put the effort in when there's no ... we're not rewarded for it and there's no incentive. Why go the trouble of having to completely re-do a course that maybe you've already got going comfortably? So I think I'm making progress. Yeah. [Interview #5, cards #80-87 of 158]

I 3
J 2
K 6

Dr. Wells' excerpt above seems to illustrate two points: (a) a possible major difference in the outcome goals of teaching using educational technology between faculty and administrators and (b) the practice of faculty to carry-out self-directed learning in at least the pedagogy of teaching using educational technology. In a previous section, Dr. Wells' motivation behind teaching using educational technology was shared: (a) personal curiosity in teaching in a different modality and the resulting satisfaction gained from the creativity and challenge of teaching in that modality and (b) a flexible and convenient option for reaching her distance students. In contrast, the administrators' motivation behind the push to offer an online master of public health (MPH) program appeared to be capitalistic: (a) to be competitive with other public health schools that offer online MPH programs and (b) to increase student enrollment. With such dissimilar motivations, the outcome goals sought in teaching using educational technology would indeed be different between the faculty and administrators and problematic for faculty who require resources and support that may seem unnecessary to administrators. This point will be revisited in Research Question 2 as a source of conflict between the different stakeholders in research universities.

A 7
B 19

Another point that surfaced in Dr. Wells' excerpt above was her practice of carrying out self-directed learning about teaching using educational technology (e.g., "And having gotten into the literature of distance delivery, I've learned that's just a horrible, horrible way to try to teach" [Interview #5, card #83 of 158]). Furthermore, because of her self-directed learning, she seemed to understand the need for faculty development (i.e., HRD) in the pedagogy of teaching at a distance: "It's a different environment and faculty need to understand that. They're going to need some training and they're going to need to do some re-thinking of their materials because a voice-over PowerPoint is not the way to go every single time" [Interview #5, card #84 of 158]. Thus, the gap to be bridged appeared to be a lack of similar knowledge in the administrators: "Yeah, yeah, it's taken some education because they were originally thinking 'well, we could grow all these students because we can just give them an online class'" [Interview #5, cards #84-85 of 158].

M2
M5b
B3
J4

Until the administrators come to understand the motivation for faculty to become engaged in teaching using educational technology, develop their knowledge base about the pedagogy of teaching using educational technology, and help create a facilitating infrastructure such as Warschauer's (2002) physical, digital, human, and social resources, the differences in the outcome goals between the faculty and administrators would appear to be a barrier in the successful implementation of teaching using educational technology. The seeming need for administrator development will be discussed under *Chapter V: Conclusions, Implications, and Recommendations.*

M2c
M5b
(1-4)

Other participants who did not have access to strong depart mental support also appeared to wish for it, as suggested by Dr. Wilson:

M5c(2)
C7

I developed some courses back years ago on overheads and with 35 mm slides and I've never converted all of that material over to PowerPoint and the new technology. So I still have a quite bit of pretty good stuff. I've scanned a lot of slides and moved them over to PowerPoint and digital images but a lot of my stuff that I had on overheads I've just kind of left it and gone on. ... It would have been nice if we had funds and support to sit down and do a lot of that but we don't. We have one technical software support person for the 15 faculty in the department with a student worker, so basically you go from having a secretarial type support for every 2-3 faculty to 1 for 16 or 17. [Interview #4, cards #82-83 of 175]

B7
C8

Another support the participants indicated would be helpful was the support for funding. Here are Dr. Reeve's thoughts:

> ... I think that departments or programs that expect web-based courses need to make that financial investment for the faculty member. To get them big enough computers, huge enough hard drive because the files are huge. I had to get a backup hard drive that sits on my desk because Camtasia will quickly use up all of my hard drive space. I personally, with salary savings, purchased the camera and the mic. ... Now for the aspiring professors, somebody who hasn't managed or doesn't have the mechanism of salary savings or the extra funds to purchase, they're going to need support from within their department because it's not cheap. The camera's 60 and the microphone's 60 as well. An extra hard drive is 300, 400. Certainly a big enough computer. It'll run you another 300, 400 in addition to what you need in terms of the overall price. So it's an investment. [Interview #9, cards #95 and 97 of 102]

Similarly, Dr. Johnston shared his views on the need for funding support to maintain his vast online database of plant images:

> Well, what's happened is that the systems that I kind of demoed for you are running mainly because of the willingness of the people from that center to keep them up. Occasionally the servers will go down, there will be like a power outage. And I'll have to kind of nudge them over there. I would tell the person that I've worked with over there, "look it'd be nice if you re-established this system." Then they'll send a student in there to get them setup. I don't know what they do. So it would be nice if there was funding to make it so that I don't have to rely on their good auspices, you know, to do this. And I kicked around

various notions of funding but at this stage of the game, I've kind of decided that it's just not worth the time and the energy to pursue it. [Interview #7, cards #94-95 of 110]

C8   Dr. Smith agreed with the need for funding but added that finding the support was not difficult from his experience:

> I've never had problems finding money. Nor have I seen anybody that's really had problems. If you had a kookie idea you may not be able to get someone to bank roll but we're not talking about needing lots of money to do anything. I need to shoot, edit, and post a Flash video. How much do you really need for that? What do you really need? You need a camera? Well we'll get you a camera. Oh you want to buy one on your own? Someone will come up with the money. Then you buy it. [Interview #1, card #66 of 159]

C13   Based on the participants' responses, the experience of teaching using educational technology seemed to yield an overall positive end result. Creativity, pedagogical tools, access to higher education for remote students, flexibility, and lifelong learning were benefits that appeared to serve as rationales and motivation to teach using educational technology. However, the participants did experience obstacles such as time constraints, steep learning curves, technical problems, and various pedagogical challenges. Support available to the participants varied. Those who seemed least burdened by teaching using educational technology appeared to be those with the most support.

D3   In interpreting the participant responses, four points surfaced. First, faculty and administrators each may have fundamentally different outcome goals for engaging in teaching using educational technology, especially in distance education. While faculty may seek creativity, improved pedagogy, improved access to higher education, flexibility, and lifelong learning, administrators may seek capital growth through increased student enrollment. This fundamental difference may contribute to conflicts in the utilities of teaching using educational technology, and this point will be addressed as a finding under *Research Question 2*.

Second, faculty may require two sets of expertise development: (a) skill development in educational technology products such as Blackboard Vista and (b) knowledge development in the pedagogy of teaching using educational technology. Furthermore, self-directed or self-paced learning may be a helpful approach for faculty because their tight schedule may impede them from participating in scheduled workshops that occur on designated dates and times.

J4   Third, administrators may also require knowledge development, chiefly, in understanding the factors that motivate faculty in teaching using educational technology and the pedagogy for teaching using educational technology. Without such knowledge, administrators seemed to develop unrealistic expectations such as shared by Dr. Wells:

> Yeah, yeah, it's taken some education because they were originally thinking "well, we could grow all these students because we can just give them an online class." No, it doesn't work that way. It's not automated so that you can put 100 students on. I think they had a vision that it was a thing, a product, that you just put out there and it sort of goes along by itself and takes care of itself. [Interview #5, cards #84-85 of 158]

E8   Fourth, the above three points are areas of concern for HRD. With the metaphors of organizational problem solver and change agent (Watkins, 2001), the field of HRD can attend to the issue of mismatched outcome goals between faculty and administrators and with further inquiry, perhaps can arrive at theories and models that appropriately address these issues. Similarly, with the metaphor of human capital developer (Watkins,

2001), HRD can address the need for faculty and administrator knowledge and expertise development in the multiple facets of teaching using educational technology. HRD's possible role in addressing these issues will be discussed further in *Chapter V: Conclusions, Implications, and Recommendations.*

The second research question—How is the experience affecting them as more demands are placed on faculty to obtain external research funds?—addressed the effects of academic capitalism on the experience of teaching using educational technology. This question is explored next.

B8   ***Research Question 2.***

How is the experience affecting them as more demands are placed on faculty to obtain external research funds?

Academic capitalism is a worldwide phenomenon where institutions of higher education engage in enterprising and marketable activities for the purpose of generating funds for the institutions through their research capacities and also by commodifying education (Bok, 2003; Brint, 2005; Deem, 2001; Etzkowitz, 2004; Etzkowitz et al., 2000; Geiger, 2004; Häyrinen-Alestalo & Peltola, 2006; Slaughter & Leslie, 1997; Slaughter & Rhoades, 2004, 2005). The pressures of academic capitalism appeared to be present at University A and University B, based on the participant responses that identified conducting research—especially, funded research—as the most important duty as a faculty member. Furthermore, because teaching is considered secondary to research, or tertiary to research and service, efforts spent on teaching, which includes teaching using educational technology, tended not to be rewarded, or if rewarded, rewarded less.

D5   Thus, the participants shared a work life marred by juggling conflicting demands. Here is Dr. Baker's experience:

There is definitely a conflict because to write a competitive grant proposal, I have to totally immerse myself in it at least a month, and during that time, I have to put a low priority to responding to my students during the time that I put into the course. Or, I end up doing it between courses and then I don't do any course prep time. And so yeah, that's one of the very dissatisfying aspects. [Interview #2, card #110 of 152]

D11   Dr. Wells' experience too depicts a work life characterized by constant juggling:

> It's the juggling. If I could just do research, or if I just teach, it's the constant juggling and the multitasking and then the administrative burden on top of that because we do teaching, we do research, and we do service and that's what we're evaluated on and it really is a constant juggling of those three and it requires a level of multitasking that really can be exhausting because what we do is so detailed. Putting a paper together, manuscript for publication, you really need to be focused. Running analyses, you need to be focused. And it's very difficult to juggle all; none of it is easy. [Interview #5, card #135 of 158]

Four themes emerged relevant to the second research question regarding the effects of academic capitalism on the faculty experience of teaching using educational technology. This section explores the four themes: (a) the professoriate in the research university, (b) promotion and tenure (P&T) guidelines/reward systems at the research university, (c) the effects of academic capitalism, and (d) the conflicts over the utilities of teaching using educational technologies.

D11
D13

The Professoriate in the Research University

The study participants described common experiences as faculty at a research university, whether at University A or University B. The common experiences pertained to the work life attributes, the primary importance placed on conducting research, and the secondary or tertiary nature of teaching. Based on these experiences, the participants shared ideas on when a faculty member should focus on teaching and imparted advice to junior faculty, the assistant professors.

E4   *Work life attributes.* The participants described research universities as work places characterized by significant independence and autonomy, although the faculty carry a heavy work load. The criteria for advancement appeared to be clear. For example, both Dr. Wells and Dr. Smith described professors as *independent contractors.* Here is what Dr. Wells said: "The way academics work, we're all a bunch of independent contractors and we could really do what we do anywhere" [Interview #5, card #120 of 158]. Similarly, Dr. Smith said: "You're an independent contractor when you're a faculty member" [Interview #1, card #74 of 159].

D13   Autonomy seems to accompany this independence, as shared by Dr. Smith: "I think it's just an amazing thing that it actually works at an institution like this university because faculty members are just autonomous units who nobody has any idea what people do" [Interview #1, card #58 of 159]. Dr. Wilson also commented about the autonomous faculty work life:

> I mean nobody checks "what have you done?" Once here, they say "what you got to bring in?" And you have a lot of direction into your job description and how you fit particularly. If you're in the system a while, you're able to. You help plan departments and curriculums and courses and carve a niche and do your thing. [Interview #4, card #38 of 175]

D10   The work load for the participants appeared to be heavy, as
D5   they were expected to conduct research, teach, and provide service. As shared previously, participants noted engaging in constant juggling and multitasking and working on activities that require great attention to detail. Dr. Wells elaborated on her thoughts on the constant juggling brought on by the work load:

> My complaint always is none of our jobs is easy. We're doing research that requires a great deal of background and

thought and creativity and staying on top of things, you can't let the publications in your field go by, you have to be reading and staying up. Same with teaching. You're in front of people, you have, even online, you have a product that you want to have at a level that you're not embarrassed about, there's a lot of juggling. [Interview #5, cards 135-136 of 158]

F1   A potential danger for faculty members appeared to be misguided time management. As a result, they may expend their efforts on less rewarding activities such as teaching, as shared by Dr. Caldwell:

> Like I said, if you're not a good manager, then you end up managing too much. I tend to do this, for the convenience of the students as opposed to making it convenient for you to get all of your work done, and so that's where I think you have to really sit down and think about how you're going to structure your week, your day, in terms of access to you personally, when you're not available. I think that's really important. And I'm slowly learning that, slowly learning how to do that. But when a student gets into trouble I tend to immediately want to work with them. [Interview #3, card #94 of 165]

D7   Thus, autonomy seems to be a distinct and appreciated characteristic of the professoriate. However, with criteria for advancement so clearly delineated and favoring faculty conducting research over teaching, the attribute of autonomy seems to be conditional.

F3   *Primary importance placed on conducting research.* When I asked how important it was for the faculty members in their departments to be conducting research, all 10 participants concurred that conducting research was very important. Responses ranged from a phrase, "very important," from Drs. Baker, Andrews, and Reeves [Interview #2, card #82 of 152; Interview #8, card #44 of 74; Interview #9, card #60 of 102] to sentences that noted the importance of conducting research even for the tenured professors. Dr. Wilson stated "Everybody. Even old guys need to be doing some" [Interview #4, card #128 of 175] and Dr. Andrews noted "the expectation is that all levels will continue to engage in research" [Interview #8, card #46 of 74].

B9
B7

However, conducting research appeared to be of the utmost importance to junior faculty such as assistant professors on the tenure track. Dr. Andrews pointed out "It's probably most important for assistant professors because they have to get tenure. That's going to be the case in every department in the university" [Interview #8, card #45 of 74]. Dr. Johnston's experience as a junior faculty during the 1980s supported this thought, although money apparently was not the primary motive back then. Rather, the motivation appeared to be a form of a "prestige maximizer" as described by Slaughter and Leslie (1997, p. 17): "Since most faculty teach, and many faculty perform public service, but fewer win competitive research funds from government or industry, research is the activity that differentiates among and within universities."

> Well as a new faculty member certainly the need for me to obtain research funds was made evident by my superiors. In those days and we're talking early '80s the notion that funding kind of gave you the stamp of approval of your peers was significant because with NSF you have review panels and you were competing against your colleagues and the money per se was not that big of a deal. It was getting a competitive research grant and at that time you know the teaching, from my point of view, I freely admit it, did not receive the focus creatively and the time and energy I invested to get the research off the ground. Mainly as my survival as an academic required that I get the research off the ground, get some funding, graduate students. Simple as that. [Interview #7, cards #78-81 of 110]

B7   Although the motive may not have been financial during the 1980s, it definitely appeared to be so today. Here are Dr. Smith's thoughts on this issue:

> But the most important thing we do is, and everybody would agree, the most important thing we do, the thing that is valued most, is research. Funded research, I'll even qualify that. Funded research would be the most important. There are lots of research we can do that is free but the university is probably not as interested in that. They want to get their cut, they want to get their indirect costs. [Interview #1, card #103 of 159]

With research, rather funded research, considered to be primary, teaching, then, appeared to be secondary, as noted above by Dr. Johnston's statement that teaching did not receive as much of his creativity and energy as that of conducting research.

B9   The next section describes the apparent secondary nature of teaching at the participants' research universities.

Secondary nature of teaching. The participants viewed teaching to be secondary or sometimes tertiary following service, as stated by Dr. Jones: "Service, probably service being second, and then teaching third, I would think" [Interview #6, card #38 of 90]. They also mentioned the lack of reward for teaching. Dr. Wells shared: "And then on the teaching side, there's really no reward for teaching. We haven't had anybody go up here for tenure on teaching" [Interview #5, #43 of 158]. Dr. Johnston added to the view of teaching as a secondary focus:

> And the spinoff basically was the teaching and that's the bottom line. There has never been any funding, at least to my knowledge, focused on teaching. It's often the case teaching is more or less the backburner thing. People are interested in doing it because people have to teach but it just kind of gets secondary funding and secondary focus. [Interview #7, card #19 of 110]

A11
A9   Furthermore, Dr. Williams shared his thoughts that those who
      teach well may be seen as focusing on the wrong activity:

> And if you teach too well, you were here for your research.
> Boy, think about how much better you'd be doing with your
> research if you weren't screwing around so much with your
> teaching. Do you really love this stuff, are you really doing
> as much as you could to be making the great discovery?
> What's going on here? [Interview #10, card #64 of 110]

B9   Perhaps because teaching is not rewarded, it is an activity
      that receives as little energy as possible, as mentioned earlier by
      Dr. Johnston from his experience as a junior faculty and here
      by Dr. Williams:

> I mean most people just ... when they think about their
> teaching they're thinking about how do I put the mini-
> mum time and energy and to not be on anybody's radar
> screen. They enjoy it, they take it seriously, but it's not real-
> ly what they're supposed to be doing so it's not what they're
> going to do. [Interview #10, card #108 of 110]

B8
B9   And to those faculty who want to focus on teaching, the advice
      may be that perhaps they should consider leaving the research
      university. Dr. Smith shared his thoughts on this point:

> Go to a community college or to other universities that are
> not as research focused as ours. Go somewhere else. Every
> job description we've had, every job description that comes
> out for faculty position at this university, has a statement
> that says something like "development of an external-
> ly-funded research project is a requirement of this job." So
> you can hope and wish and pray that wasn't it once you got
> here and you're a failure at it but that's still the expectation
> of the job. If you don't like it, go somewhere else. There are
> plenty of jobs, jobs that pay well.
> [Interview #1, card #114 of 159]

This advice appeared to be significant to the current doctoral students whose career plans may include joining the professoriate at research universities.

B6   The findings from *Research Question 1* included the rationales (i.e., personal satisfaction in the creativity, flexibility, and lifelong learning of teaching using educational technology) that served as motivations for the participants to engage in teaching using educational technology. Based on the findings of *Research Question 2* that depict the utmost importance of conducting funded research, I pause to wonder how strong the personal satisfactions they experienced must have been for them to engage in teaching using educational technology when the criteria for advancement at research universities clearly appeared to place teaching at a tier lower than conducting funded research.

When to focus on teaching. Thus, with teaching apparently viewed to be secondary to research or tertiary to research and service, the participants noted when faculty at research universities would typically focus on teaching: after receiving tenure and being promoted to associate professor. Dr. Smith offered his views on this point:

> I'd say that's something you wait until you're already promoted and tenured to deal with just because it consumes so much time and the university has no way of categorizing those efforts and no way of rewarding the faculty member at all. So it's really interesting. I think you're going to hear this over and over and over again. [Interview #1, card #41 of 159]

B5   However, four of my study participants who focus on teaching are long-time full professors: Dr. Wilson, Dr. Jones, Dr. Johnston, and Dr. Andrews. In fact, Dr. Johnston made the following statement:

> I can afford to do this stuff because I'm old and I'm not, you know, I'm a full professor. I have some latitude that I didn't

have when I was 35 and associate prof. But for the younger people, they don't have that luxury. Certainly I didn't before I was full professor. [Interview #7, card #56 of 110]

B7   Furthermore, I asked Dr. Wilson, the faculty member who chose to focus on teaching after recovering from a car accident and realizing his research program needed to be restarted, and who subsequently informed his department chair his intentions were to focus on teaching, the following question:

> Researcher: So do you think you can say that to your department head because you're tenured or because you're a full professor? Obviously an assistant professor couldn't say that to a department head.
>
> Dr. Wilson: Nope.
>
> Researcher: Would an associate professor be able to say that?
>
> Dr. Wilson: I wouldn't recommend it.

Therefore, although a faculty member could start to focus on teaching once tenured and promoted to associate professor, perhaps those who aspire to become full professors may not be motivated to focus on teaching until they reach a full professorship. This possibility of faculty delaying their focus on teaching raises a point concerning *who* is teaching the students of a research university such as University A. Based on the institutional records of University A, it is one of the top ten in size in the US. Furthermore, the Fall 2007 enrollment profile indicated an undergraduate student population that exceeded 30,000. The Fall 2006 records—the most current data available—indicated 3,875 total number of faculty members at University A. It is interesting to note that the number (n=1,929) of teaching assistants and other faculty—presumably non-tenure track faculty—is roughly half of the faculty workforce and suggests perhaps they are the ones who can focus on teaching while tenured faculty and those on tenure-track (n=1,946) must focus on conducting funded research. This point is revisited again in *Chapter V: Conclusions, Implications, and Recommendations*, when this study's implications for students are discussed.

B7
B9
    Advice to junior faculty. Because teaching is secondary or tertiary in importance, some participants cautioned junior faculty from becoming too involved in teaching, especially teaching using educational technology that requires much investment in time. Dr. Smith shared his advice:

> I would caution any junior faculty member to restrict any teaching …. Teach as little as humanly possible. And certainly don't teach in a manner that consumes additional time like shooting and editing videos and doing stuff like that. Just grab your notes and go teach. Be pleasant and polite. I think that's pretty good advice. [Interview #1, card #44 of 159]

B9
    Dr. Wells also shared her views on junior faculty and teaching:

> The challenge with junior faculty is it takes so much work to develop a course and my experience has been that until you've taught it at least three times, it's just a lot of work because you tend to be developing it the first year. You're usually just a class or two ahead of your lecture because you're putting all the materials together. The second year, you're kind of roughing out, smoothing out the edges. And the third year, you're feeling pretty confident that you've found the things that work. You've got exams that work, you've got homework. So after about three years, it becomes a matter of keeping current and probably putting it ...
>
> In the semester where you've got a brand new course, you don't have a lot of time left over. You always have service responsibilities. There are committees that you have to serve on. Then you've got to keep your research rolling along and then you probably have to get grant proposals. You have to kind of always have that cycle going. And, for junior faculty, all of that's coming together while they're

developing their skills, the skills that are for that. So it's really really rough the first two years as an assistant. Because you are spending a lot of time developing your coursework and then you have people mentoring you telling you "don't spend so much time, you're not going to get tenure on your class work, you're not going to get tenure on education." [Interview #5, cards # 56, 58-60 of 158]

A4   Even so, two of the study participants focused on teaching early on as assistant professors and recently were promoted: Dr. Reeves to associate professor and Dr. Smith to full professor. I asked if there was a conflict in managing the research and teaching demands. Here is Dr. Reeves' response: "I don't know. I just have managed and maybe it's just a quirk, I've been the exception but I managed to get it done" [Interview #9, card #87 of 102]. Perhaps, the endeavor to focus on research as well as teaching just simply entails devoting more hours to work. Here is Dr. Smith's response to my question regarding the conflict between research and teaching demands:

> No conflict. I don't have a conflict. Just do it. If I was to choose, if they limited the amount of time I work, if I didn't work 60, 70, or 80 hours a week, and worked a regular 40-hour work week, all my work would be focused on my research. [Interview #1, cards #119-120 of 159].

A3   In summary, the professoriate in the research university appeared to be characterized by independence and autonomy with faculty carrying a heavy work load doing research, teaching, and providing service. However, the successful path to promotion and tenure appeared to be very clear in that conducting funded research is most important and teaching is secondary or tertiary. For this reason, the independence and autonomy attributes appeared to be conditional: a faculty member at a research university perhaps is most autonomous if he or she is first and foremost a productive awardee of funded research. Below is an excerpt that illustrates this point:

Researcher: How important is it for faculty members in your department to be conducting research?

Dr. Baker: 100%.

Researcher: Very important?

Dr. Baker: Very important.

Researcher: And do most of them abide by this importance?

Dr. Baker: Yes, they lose their job if they don't.

Researcher: So their job is dependent on conducting research?

Dr. Baker: Yeah.

The advice for junior faculty included spending the least amount of effort as possible on teaching. Earlier in this chapter I had mentioned that I was unable to recruit assistant professors as my study participants. Given the advice for junior faculty to devote the least amount of effort on teaching, I can understand and appreciate their reluctance in engaging in a dissertation study such as mine that would have offered no reward toward their advancement as a professor. The next segment explores the promotion and tenure guidelines and reward system as noted by the participants.

A2   *Promotion and Tenure Guidelines/Reward System at the Research University*

Not surprisingly, given the views shared by the participants in the previous section, all 10 participants stated that the reward system at their respective university values conducting research the most. Dr. Smith shared his thoughts:

> Because it's easier to get promoted based on doing, conducting, securing external funds, and publishing research. If you do that, you have a much greater likelihood of getting promoted than if you teach. People understand that. How many did you have? You had 18 journal articles and a million dollars in grants? You're promoted. What did you do? Oh you had average teaching evaluations and you

wrote 1 journal article? I don't know what to do with you. [Interview #1, card #130 of 159]

A7   Furthermore, some colleges and departments appeared to have established a minimum funding their faculty members are expected to garner, such as in Dr. Wells' and Dr. Reeves' college. Dr. Reeves shared her college's guidelines:

> We're expected to raise 25% of our salary. There is an expectation that we will be involved in research projects that credit us with the salary support equal to 25% of our salary. That's the benchmark and sometimes you meet it and sometimes we far exceed it. Some faculty are sold out at 80% of their time. For example, this past year, I was at some points at 40% and one grant ended and went down to 15% and then within a month back up at 30%. [Interview #9, cards #60-61 of 10]

A6
A11   For Dr. Baker, the expectations are that she brings in "triple digit grants … like hundreds of thousands of dollars" [Interview #2, card #104 of 152]. For Dr. Caldwell, the requirements are as follows:

> … the dean in our college has said that in the next two years we are going to be weaned off of much of any support from them and if our research brings in less than 25% overhead, we don't get any of that return. The dean sweeps it all. So people in our research department have to get grants that have over 25% overhead in order for any of that overhead to come back to the department to help defray cost to the department. [Interview #3, cards #2-3 of 165]

However, the possibility of conducting educational research appeared to be dependent on the field with which the faculty were associated. For some science fields, conducting educational research appeared to be considered out of the ordinary. During our interview, I mentioned to Dr. Johnston that the research university did not seem to reward faculty for teaching. His response to my statement is shown below:

Unless you can frame it up as research. And some people do that. But it's very difficult especially if you have a history of doing research, hard core research. ... I think it's unusual for somebody like a chemist or a botanist or what have you to do a research thing on teaching. And it mostly comes from folks like you. [Interview #7, cards #106-107 of 110]

A11   In summary, the reward system at a research university appeared to be unmistakably based on the ability to conduct externally funded research. Consequently, some colleges and departments seemed to have begun to establish minimum requirements concerning how much funding a faculty member should generate, although the minimum requirements seemed to be different for each college or department, perhaps based on the viability of the department's or college's field to be successful in academic capitalism. Thus, participants offered different strategies they have carried out in order to be successfully funded when the success rate is so low and when certain fields are not amenable to academic capitalism. The next section explores the effects of academic capitalism.

A11   **Effects of Academic Capitalism**

As stated by all participants, the push to obtain external research funds in a research university is strong. For example, Dr. Jones' department extends annual reminders to assistant and associate professors:

Oh, very strong push. We have an annual meeting with the non-tenured faculty members, tenure track but they haven't received tenure yet, and the department head and I meet with everyone, with the assistant and associate professors. Big pushes on funding. [Interview #6, cards #58 of 90]

B1   A common subtheme that emerged regarding academic capitalism, besides the push to obtain funding, was the emphasis placed on obtaining funds from agencies that award larger indirect or overhead fees. Another subtheme was how the funds awarded were spent: to support the faculty, their research programs, and their graduate students. A final subtheme was the perspective of distance education as an instance of academic capitalism.

A8   *Indirect or overhead costs.* Indirect costs, also referred to as overhead costs, appeared to be the monies an institution collected from a funding agency in return for research being conducted at the institution. This fee was in addition to the salary and other support a researcher had requested from the agency. Participants indicated that the push to generate funds also included obtaining funds from agencies noted for paying higher percentages of indirect costs. Below is an excerpt of my interview with Dr. Jones regarding the indirect costs:

> Researcher: I've heard this from other departments that faculty members are encouraged to go for agencies that have high indirect costs or indirect fees, is that true here too?
>
> Dr. Jones: Sure, oh absolutely.
>
> Researcher: NSF I think has a high ...
>
> Dr. Jones: Oh, you bet. Because that's the payback the university gets. It's like 40—50% on top of and they get the mass of it. A little bit comes back to the college and then the college gives a little bit back to the department but most of it goes to the university. [Interview #6, card #60 of 90]

A6
A8   Dr. Caldwell's statement was shared earlier of her dean's expectations for faculty to receive grant awards from agencies that pay at least 25% in indirect costs. She elaborated on this point:

> Researcher: How important is it for faculty members in your department to be conducting research?
>
> Dr. Caldwell: Yes, well, absolutely. There's no question. In fact, like we were talking about, the direction is to get a particular kind of research done in terms of source of

funding so that it carries, or it can bear, a large overhead of return.

Researcher: And 25% is the minimum?

Dr. Caldwell: I believe that is right, at least that's what somebody told me yesterday, 25% is the minimum. Most NSF grant will be like 45% overhead. What would happen is the dean would take the first 25% and the next 20% would come back to the department. That's generally the way it works. [Interview #3, cards #100-101 of 165]

A11   The consequences of receiving funds that pay smaller indirect costs appeared to affect the operating budget of the department or college. Dr. Caldwell continued her thoughts on this point:

> Many of our professors have been getting by, quote unquote, you know with state funded grants or US Fish and Wildlife grants that only allow 15—20% overhead and basically we cannot run our program. In fact, that's one of the reasons why we started running low on funds in our department in the last few years because costs went up and income was not coming in. So, our new department head has said basically we want people doing high dollar overhead research to be able to support our program. Otherwise we probably won't get any money for new positions or anything like that. [Interview #3, card #4 of 165]

A10   Dr. Johnston reflected on the funding he received to develop the online database of images of vascular plants. Because it was awarded by the state's higher education coordinating board, the funding did not include indirect costs. Here are his thoughts on having worked on that grant with no indirect costs:

> And I was, again, where I didn't have to worry too much about satisfying the administration's need for indirect costs, to be quite frank with you. Even in '95 I could afford to kind of get a small grant. The coordinating board didn't pay indirect costs to our university but there was some

prestige because what we got our archrival didn't get so they were happy about that. But they probably weren't too happy about the fact, at least from what I saw, there was no heavy indirect costs. If I was doing NSF work, they would be getting almost half of the proposal's value in indirect costs. [Interview #7, cards 62-63 of 110]

A9
B2   ***External funds support faculty, research programs,***
D5   ***and graduate students.***

Besides the indirect costs, a grant award appeared to contain funds that support faculty, their research program, and their graduate students. Faculty may require funding support during the summer months if they are on a 9-month appointment, as in the case for the faculty in Dr. Jones' department:

> One other big motivation, everyone in this department is on a 9-month contract except for the department head and me. Everyone else is on 9-month. And there is very little summer teaching so if they want support, they have to get the grants. We give summer support for the first two years of all new appointments. So they're given two years to transition into the grant-getting but after that, they have to get grants if they want more than a 9-month salary. And of course, the tenure process demands it also. I don't think anyone gets tenure at this place anymore unless you get grants, at least in the college of science. [Interview #6, card #48-49 of 90]

B2   Dr. Williams repeated the point of external funds supporting faculty summer salary (and more):

> ... But the summer salaries come from the grant, the salaries for the postdocs and the salaries for the graduate students and travel and conferences and such come from the grants. [Interview #10, card #75 of 110]

B3   Dr. Caldwell described how the graduate students are supported by externally awarded funds in her department:

> ... if you bring in a graduate student, you need to have funding assured for that student. You just can't say "Oh gee, I'd love to have that person as a student." Unless you've got a research grant that's going to employ them as a research assistantship, you can't bring them in. You got to have a way to support them. [Interview #3, cards #113-114 of 165]

C14   And, the ability to generate external funds appeared to be connected to the development of graduate programs. Dr. Caldwell continued:

> By and large each faculty is supposed to get their research grant funds for their program, for their students. So we don't have a fall back to fill in the gaps and we have a small ability to do that. If a student can't get money to support themselves, it makes it very hard to build a graduate program if you can't do that. [Interview #3, card #119 of 165]

Dr. Johnston's approach to funding students was to fund them jointly with the university:

> The better funded program is going to fund its graduate students. If you're writing a proposal in science and usually it's going to be to NIH or NSF, having in your budget money for graduate students ... My personal approach was to fund graduate students in the summer time and let the university fund them in the winter time for economy. And also for a graduate student their only opportunity to teach is being a teaching assistant or working with labs and teaching in the summer and the winter time. I think there were a few situations where I would fund a graduate student fully in their first year and their last year but tried to make sure that they got some teaching in. [Interview #7, card #82 of 110]

C14   Dr. Williams spoke of the graduate and postdoc students he supported through external research funds:

I have been supporting ... I've got two and half, depending on how you do the counting, two and a half at the moment. And one postdoc but I often have a lot of other teaching activities which I have the students who do research for me do these research projects on the side so in some sense it's teaching research but that's how I support them. At the moment I have four students, four graduate students in one capacity or another. That's unusual. I've got one who is going to graduate in August and is going to Penn as a post-doc so I'm going to lose him pretty soon. And two others just started so .... Two is probably more of a typical number. [Interview #10, card #78 of 110]

C14   *Distance education.* In addition to the indirect costs and external funds that support faculty, their research program, and their graduate students, another subtheme pertaining to academic capitalism included pressure from the administration for faculty to engage in distance education because of the possible revenue that can be generated through the distance education fees. In some cases, the revenue seemed to trickle down to the faculty and served as incentives.

B15   Dr. Wells shared the pressure for her college to engage in distance education:

But in talking with other faculty, I think they're going to be ... There's a big move, and again this gets back to the whole business part of the deal, to be competitive with online programs. We have an MPH [master of public health] and there are a variety of universities that now offer completely online MPHs. So we have pressure from above to find a way to compete in that market. [Interview #5, card #32 of 158]

B15   Dr. Wilson also has seen the pressure to engage in distance education emerge in his department, apparently driven by pressure from the legislature:

There's been this thing from the institution, from the top down, legislature said we need to offer more distance courses so administrators are running around "we need more distance courses." [Interview #4, card #101 of 175]

C14
B18
B19

And, perhaps this pressure is economic in nature as suggested by Dr. Wilson:

Dr. Wilson: ... We can't continue to support the escalating cost of education, I don't think, ad infinitum. So at some point it's going to have to be an economic consideration.

Researcher: So do you think, at least in your department, the push for distance ed is ...

Dr. Wilson: And that's economic driven. Absolutely. They don't want to have to bring all the students in here to campus.

Researcher: The building space?

Dr. Wilson: Building space and cost. If you can stay home and work at a job and take courses at the same time, you'll be busy earning salary and paying taxes and not up here sitting in an apartment going to classes and sitting in a classroom. It shifts education away from the intensive, on-campus experience into a more disseminated spread over time combined with work type experience. [Interview #4, card #115-116 of 175]

B18
B19

At the departmental level, the motivation to engage in distance education appears to include a monetary reason. In addition to the service or "altruistic motivation" [Interview #6, card #8 of 90] of offering an online master's program in statistics to students who cannot participate in a face-to-face program, Dr. Jones explained the monetary benefit his department will receive by teaching at a distance:

But there is a monetary one, too. The department will receive some financial benefits, direct financial benefits, from the fees paid by the DL students. So there is some financial also. [Interview #6, card #9 of 90]

B10   Faculty, in turn, appear to receive financial incentives, such as shared by Dr. Baker: "One of the motivators for me to teach through distance education is that I actually get funds back that I can use in whatever I need to" [Interview #2, card #15 of 152]. Likewise, Dr. Caldwell shared the financial incentive she received for teaching at a distance:

> Dr. Caldwell: I'm getting a little bit of research money funds for developing distance technology capabilities for some of these courses.
>
> Researcher: And where do you get those funds from?
>
> Dr. Caldwell: Well, it came from the dean. And then the funds to employ the people who are helping me to do this are through the dean as well. But this time I got it directly. It's only about $6000, but I can use that for anything. I can buy software, I can hire a graduate student, I can buy equipment, I can spend it however I feel like I need to add that distance capability, web/online distance capability to my class. [Interview #3, card #49 of 165]

C12   *Conflicts Over the Utilities of Teaching Using*
C10   *Educational Technologies*

B10   The fourth subtheme that emerged under the effects of academic capitalism is the apparent conflicts that arose—chiefly between the faculty and administrators—regarding the utilities of teaching using educational technologies in a performance system (i.e., research university) that places a high importance on faculty's ability to conduct funded research. And, the conflict seemed to be exacerbated when the administrators, who appeared to lack an expertise or knowledge about teaching using educational technology, viewed distance education as an opportunity to be competitive in their respective education markets and to generate additional revenues through increased student enrollments and the resulting distance education fees. For example, Dr. Wells' comments earlier regarding her college's vision to be competitive in the online MPH market expressed an unrealistic expectations set by the administrators:

> Yeah, yeah, it's taken some education because they were originally thinking "well, we could grow all these students because we can just give them an online class." No, it doesn't work that way. It's not automated so that you can put 100 students on. I think they had a vision that it was a thing, a product, that you just put out there and it sort of goes along by itself and takes care of itself. No, it's still class requiring faculty time, you can't just have a bunch more distance cohorts and expect one person to now have a class of 100. First of all, you need to cap it. I don't know how you do more than 20 meaningfully. Probably 15's better at a graduate level. So you can't have a 60-person class. You'd be doing nothing but reading emails all day. So I think I've gotten them backed up to realizing there are a lot of limitations and it's not a magic answer to growth in the school. [Interview #5, cards #85-86 of 158]

B13　　　In contrast, Dr. Wells' motivation to engage in teaching using educational technology did not appear to be financial at all. Rather it appeared to be the personal satisfaction that resulted from the creativity and challenge of teaching in that modality as well as the flexibility of not having to teach at night. Therefore, for other faculty members who may not be personally motivated, convincing them to engage in distance education would seem to be difficult:

> And they're going to have to convince faculty that it's worth their time, especially tenured faculty. Why would they put the effort in when there's no ... we're not rewarded for it and there's no incentive. Why go the trouble of having to completely re-do a course that maybe you've already got going comfortably? [Interview #5, card #87 of 158]

B19   One perspective of this conflict in mismatched motivations
C12   and outcome expectations may be due to not taking into con-
C9   sideration the motivations, outcome expectations, and concerns
of the *multiple* stakeholders. While the faculty may be motivated
by the desire to excel in meaningful scholarship and teaching,
the administrators may be motivated by the need to accrue
operating funds through external research monies with large
indirect costs. With such mismatched motivations, the outcomes expected by each would understandably be different.

C9   The business ethics literature offers the multi-fiduciary stakeholder theory (Goodpaster, 1991) for taking into consideration
the needs of *all* stakeholders. According to this theory, in addition to the stockholders, businesses can affect and are affected by multiple stakeholders such as the employees, vendors,
competitors, communities, and countries, and should weigh in
the needs of the different parties equally. Likewise, in the phenomena of academic capitalism and teaching using educational
technology, multiple stakeholders appear to be present and at
least include the faculty and administrators and perhaps even
the legislature. Taking into consideration the motivations and
outcomes expected by *all* stakeholders in regards to effectively
teaching using educational technology, being successful in academic capitalism may be necessary. Without such an approach,
conflicts such as the following may continue to be present:

> Dr. Johnston: … This business of commercialization has
> been a constant kind of thing. … Like the fact that we put
> 30,000 images online has attracted attention. The systems
> that we have in place have been in place for a long time.
> And they're quite googleable because Google has been
> picking them up for a long time. And there is among many
> faculty these days kind of an entrepreneurial approach to
> things. So there is, … although it's not a direct kind of a
> pressure, to try to make some money out of the operation.
> Throwing some commercials or something so that it could

be self-sustaining. There is also on the other side of the coin, and again this is not a direct item, but forces from the administration that indicate you shouldn't maybe be supplying all this stuff for free where anybody can utilize it and everybody does.

Researcher: Because it's not password protected at the moment?

Dr. Johnston: No, it's open, to my knowledge anyway. And you have those dynamics in play with regard to what I think maybe the topic of your research is probably. My notion is I'm a public employee and I am reticent to have the public pay twice for what I do. But there a lot of people, especially locally, that kind of would like to put a charge on it somehow. Put a constraint, have somebody register etcetera etcetera. And I'm not sure about WebCT or the systems they have in play now for faculty but I have a feeling you'll have to register to log in.

Researcher: Right, it's not open to the world.

Dr. Johnston: Right. Right. And I've kind of been waiting for them to pressure me into rolling this stuff into that sort of a format. The fact that it's so anomalous, it was started so early on, people probably don't know about it, you have two institutions involved, that center and us and what have you, they just haven't done it. But there's that dynamic in play that relates to I think what you're up to. [Interview #7, cards #98-102 of 110]

C9
C12
D3

The excerpt below describes another conflict:

Researcher: So then how is your job satisfaction affected by your efforts to teach using educational technology and obtain ...

Dr. Baker: It's actually been improved because when I'm dissatisfied with what's happening at the department level, I immerse myself in the details of the technology and I enjoy it. And I feel successful. I get immediate rewards.

Researcher: So teaching is what you love, of course that's not enough, and so you do the research piece ...

Dr. Baker: Because that's what I'm evaluated on. But I could also very happily just do the research. I could be very happy in a research position.

Researcher: So then it's the kind of money you need to bring in that seems to be the weight on your shoulders.

Dr. Baker: The weight on my shoulders is it's entirely me individually. So this goes back to the capitalism thing. It's like if you have someone who's an entrepreneur, those entrepreneurs are going to be more successful if they're backed by certain infrastructure that's clearly targeted towards that success. But no, our model is that each individual faculty member is like an empire builder of their own. So they're expected to do the PR, the schmoozing, they're expected to actually write and submit and do all the details of not only the grant proposals but also the publications, they're expected to mentor the students, and the graduate students. You end up paying the graduate students to do the research because you don't have the time to do the research but then the graduate student doesn't have the experience and the training that's necessary to do the research right and so that ends up being a little mismatch there too. Then the teaching ends up being on top of that and really is not even considered in terms of evaluations unless you do poorly. [Interview #2, cards #114-118 of 152]

D1   In summary, thus far, the participants' experiences seemed to indicate that they reap a variety of benefits from teaching using educational technology. In turn, those benefits appeared to serve as rationales or motivation to teach using educational technology even though they faced various barriers such as time constraints, steep learning curves, technical problems, and pedagogical challenges.

C14   Furthermore, the participants' experiences portrayed the professorship in the research university as an independent and autonomous position. However, it is a position with a heavy work load that required a constant juggling of different tasks. The path to successful promotion and tenure in the professoriate appeared to be clearly marked by guidelines that require research productivity through external funds, and therefore, may render the autonomy of the professoriate conditional based on the ability to be successful awardee of external funds. Teaching appeared to be secondary.

D2   With a low success rate for obtaining external funding, participants appeared to make use of different strategies to aid them. The participants also spoke of the importance of large indirect costs from external funds that supplement an institution's operating budget. The grant fund itself seemed to be used to support the faculty, their research programs, and their graduate students. Engaging in distance education served a dual purpose: (a) an altruistic gesture to reach out to potential students who for various reasons cannot become residential students and (b) a monetary gain to the department and perhaps to the faculty from the distance fees paid by the students.

D5   Viewed through the perspective of the multi-fiduciary stake
H7b(2)   holder theory (Goodpaster, 1991) that suggests in addition to the stockholders, organizations can affect and are affected by multiple stakeholders such as the employees, vendors, competitors, communities, and countries, perhaps an avenue to dissolve the apparent conflicts in mismatched motivations and outcome expectations between the faculty and administrators, and even the legislature, would require taking into account the goals and expectations of each stakeholder. The last research question examines the participants' job satisfaction. That section is next.

C6   *Research Question 3.*
How is the experience affecting their job satisfaction?

The participants shared a demanding work life that was characterized by constant juggling and multitasking. Therefore, I was surprised that the majority of the participants stated they were very satisfied with their jobs. Six stated they were highly satisfied with or enjoyed being a professor, three participants were mixed in their responses, and only one stated her satisfaction was low. Some said being a professor was a dream job. Even so, all ten stated they had turnover intentions to leave University A or B at one point or another in the past, although perhaps not the professoriate. However, only two participants appeared to have recent turnover intentions. Many said teaching using educational technology was personally satisfying.

B18
E7
E4
     Because each participant's job satisfaction level and the determinants that affect it appeared to be a personal story, the details of each participant's job satisfaction will be shared as a narrative. Each narrative will start with a brief summary of my interpretation of their job satisfaction followed by a compiled version of their words. The participants are listed in the order in which they were interviewed.

Larry Smith, Interview #1

Dr. Smith, although highly satisfied with his job and University A, frequently thinks about leaving the institution. He makes his turnover intentions public and updates his curriculum vitae weekly. He has received offers but intends to stay for the right offer package. His reasons for leaving would be to move closer to his family and for more money. Teaching using educational technology and being awarded grant funds contribute to his job satisfaction.

> I like the freedom I'm given to use educational technologies in the classroom. I think taking that away I would probably be less happy, so less satisfied. I think also when

you have external funds, having money—whoever said that money doesn't buy happiness is poor, the saying goes. To have resources to do what you want to do at universities is awfully important. You get to travel, you get to buy equipment, you get to hire graduate students, that's why I'm here. So, yes. So both those things increase my satisfaction. ... Every day. I think about it [leaving] all the time. I apply for jobs all the time. I've interviewed for several department head positions. Haven't left. I keep my options open all the time. I tell people that you should always look for better opportunities to better yourself. This institution doesn't wake up every day and say how can we make Larry Smith motivated and happy so I have to wake up every morning and say how do I keep myself motivated and happy. I just got a call last week, somebody asked me to consider a position at a different university. ... It's been a long time since I've been home near my parents and brothers and stuff. I left home about 25 years ago and have been gone for a long time. To get closer to home would be good. In fact, I just applied for a position couple weeks ago. But part of it is where I am in my career. It's hard. I've had some offers and they just couldn't come up with the right package to make me move. While I'm here, I'm as loyal as I can be. I love this university, it's a great place. But they're not waking up trying to make me happy every day. That's me. My wife and I. Trying to make sure our family is happy. Every place is a great place. ... I update my vita every week because if an opportunity comes open, I want to do it. ... I also want to keep pressure on the administration. If somebody makes me a job offer for more money, I want the administration here to offer me more money to stay, right? It's the only way you can find out what you're worth. They get to put pressure on you, you should put pressure back. And if they don't want you, you should leave. [cards #123-124, 139-146 of 159]

D11 *Erica Baker, Interview #2*

D5 Dr. Baker's job satisfaction level is very low. The contributors to this low satisfaction level include her departmental culture as well as the manner in which academic capitalism is expected to be practiced at her institution—for her to become an entrepreneur without the necessary infrastructural support. However, teaching using educational technology is a source of positive job satisfaction. Dr. Baker has thought about leaving University A but has resolved to stay. She appears to be happy with her new department chair.

> My job satisfaction is very low. … I think it's primarily in terms of how people see me and the feedback that I get back from people as to how they see me. I feel that things that are important to me are not communicated to the people who evaluate me. … It's actually been improved because when I'm dissatisfied with what's happening at the department level, I immerse myself in the details of the technology and I enjoy it. And I feel successful. I get immediate rewards. … The weight on my shoulders is it's entirely me individually. So this goes back to the capitalism thing. It's like if you have someone who's an entrepreneur, those entrepreneurs are going to be more successful if they're backed by certain infrastructure that's clearly targeted towards that success. But no, our model is that each individual faculty member is like an empire builder of their own. So they're expected to do the PR, the schmoozing, they're expected to actually write and submit and do all the details of not only the grant proposals but also the publications, they're expected to mentor the students, and the graduate students. You end up paying the graduate students to do the research because you don't have the time to do the research but then the graduate student doesn't have the experience and the training that's necessary to do the research right and so that ends up being a little mismatch there too. Then the teaching ends up being on top of that and really is not even considered in terms of evaluations unless you do poorly.

... Because within my college ... it's a military leadership model rather than a business leadership model. So what I see is in academia even though the capitalization has occurred, the business knowledge of how to do things and how to organize things to get them done has not filtered into the people who are being asked to do those kinds of things. I mean it's a simple business organizational strategy type of stuff. The really ironic thing is that we have all this knowledge on this campus but it's all going into publications rather than improving how we ourselves are doing things and training our students to do things more efficiently and more effectively and more flexibly in terms of chasing where the pots of money appear and disappear and reappear. [cards #112-125 of 152]

D4
C14
D2

Sheryl Caldwell, Interview #3

After having been through several different careers, the professorship is her dream job, Dr. Caldwell said, even if it is a difficult one. However, I sensed ambivalence in her responses and wondered if they were due to the elements that lowered her job satisfaction level, such as the apparent lack of academic enthusiasm among some of her students. Indeed, I asked her about the issue of students and that seemed to contribute to lowering her job satisfaction.

She has had turnover intentions and has also wondered if she would be happier at a teaching institution. However, she has resolved to stay for she finds satisfaction in conducting research as well as teaching. She also finds satisfaction in teaching using educational technology and obtaining external research funds.

It's sort of asking myself is this what I want to do? When things do get frustrating and you think all these students nowadays blah blah blah they're not wanting to learn or it's usually in the classroom where I get depressed because probably one of the main reasons I actually came back and got my PhD and wanted to work at a university was I love learning. I am definitely a lifelong learner and I don't understand why other people wouldn't want to be too. ... Because I've had other jobs. I've had other jobs where I was totally in research, totally worked in the lab, and didn't have that educational component, and I think that really truly this is my dream job, although it's not easy. ... So right now, I like what we're doing. And I'm loving the people that I'm meeting here at the university in terms of sharing information about technology and teaching and education. That's an exciting whole new area that's keeping me jazzed up. The more I can translate that into augmenting my research program, the happier I'm going to be. So long as I can do that, I'm pretty much going to stay here. And also, I think part of it is being seen as valuable. We have a new department head now and he's put me on some committees that, like the assessment committee, I'm on the undergraduate affairs committee, I'm the faculty advisor for a fisheries group and that sort of thing, those are the kinds of things that I enjoy doing .... [cards #149-162 of 165]

D2   *Jonathan Wilson, Interview #4*

D3   Dr. Wilson is very satisfied with his job and receives personal
D13   satisfaction from teaching using educational technology. He
E4   did have turnover intentions in the 1980s. As someone who has been with the department for 50 years, including his undergraduate student years, he seems to find great satisfaction in having shaped, and in the opportunities to further shape, the curricula for his department.

> Great [job satisfaction]. If it's not, I'm going to get out of here. ... Well, yeah, there's the competition [in focusing on teaching using educational technology and obtaining external funds] but I've chosen to work with the ed tech group to develop that and I get personal satisfaction out of doing that. ... In the '80s, I thought about it enough to apply for a department head's position and got up to

the point of the second interview and decided the reason I wanted out of here was because of the administrative things that I was getting involved in: the clarity to realize I didn't want a full-time administrative job. So instead I stayed here and got out of most of the administrative stuff. I cleared it out. And administration is not my thing. I got back to teaching and research. Focused on research, and at that point, I was getting the grants and the graduate students and the post docs along with a base of fairly good load of teaching. Nothing like I have now. And it was a balance between teaching and research. And then I had the wreck. ... One of the things that I did as a president was I got our accreditation for the discipline revised. Our forestry is in the process of making major revisions, and in theirs, it's going the same way we did. And the whole discipline of forest science, rangeland ecology, and management have a potential to come together in the 21st century under natural resources with the clean distinctions that were developed in the 20th century coming back into a more integrated systems approach. And to have an opportunity to work in that is, that and working with the students on a one-to-one basis and mentoring students, is driving me professionally now. So I've got that high level professional thing of impacting things so I got myself put back on our society's accreditation panel. I'll have a policy role there as well as in the department. I've got a hand in both sides where I can have a very strong personal influence in how this thing develops over the next few years and I like that. Tried to do some of that in research, have done, and still following up. Some of the things that I've done I think are fairly innovative in decision support systems. [cards #148-158 of 175]

E3   *Theresa Wells, Interview #5*

D4
C8   Dr. Wells said her job satisfaction level was medium. The factor that lowers her satisfaction level is the constant juggling

between the multiple roles of conducting research, teaching, and providing service. She has had turnover intentions but having been in other positions, she finds the professoriate an ideal match for her. The freedom and autonomy inherent in the professoriate are rewarding.

> It's the juggling. If I could just do research, or if I just teach, it's the constant juggling and the multitasking and then the administrative burden on top of that because we do teaching, we do research, and we do service and that's what we're evaluated on and it really is a constant juggling of those three and it requires a level of multitasking that really can be exhausting because what we do is so detailed. ... What I worry about with constantly juggling all this is "am I mediocre in everything" where as if I could focus maybe I could actually be really good at one of them. ... Why do I? [choose to be in a position that requires constant juggling] Why do I ... I'm not sure what else I would do. I've come through ... in my life I've usually worked at jobs for about five years and figured out everything there is about them that I'm interested in and then I've moved on, but academics is so different because you get that stupid tenure thing and once you have tenure it's very difficult to step out of it and say "okay, now I want to go try something completely different." And there are a lot of rewards to being an academic. There's the freedom to largely choose how you want to spend your day. And the creativity of research, there's always that hope that you might make a difference, something that you're working on might someday prevent childhood cancers. That's a huge carrot out there. I haven't been able to think of another profession that, another way to structure the skills that I have that would be as much fun or as rewarding as what I'm doing, but at the same time it's one of the more frustrating jobs I've ever had. ... I keep telling my husband "let's just go be organic farmers." Although neither of us actually has ever farmed and has no clue how we could do it. But we have books and stuff, they're on the

shelf for "okay when I've had enough, we're going to go do organic farming in Virginia where it has four seasons." The chair and I used to laugh about franchises. "We just have to find the right franchising and we're out of here." She used to come in about once a month "bagels, what about bagels. The one good bagel shop closed down, they really need a good bagel shop in this town." I think like any other job there are pros and cons. I like the freedom. It's addictive. And really I don't have a boss and that gets pretty addictive too. Yeah, once you have tenure, really, nobody can make you do anything. It really relies on good will and so that's really ... and salary's nice. It's a decent salary. I have this luxurious office as you can tell, with a window view of some weird view of the parking lot, I see who's coming and who's going. ... Like I mentioned, I've really enjoyed moving to an online environment. I think it has made ... I was on the edge of burnout with teaching that class and it has actually made it fun for me again to do that. So that's the positive. [cards #135-142 of 158]

C9　　*Peter Jones, Interview #6*

C10　　Dr. Jones started to state that he very much enjoys his job but asked me to clarify my question, whether I meant his overall job satisfaction or his job satisfaction mediated through the efforts of teaching using educational technology. I replied that I viewed those two aspects of job satisfaction as the same because dissatisfaction brought on by teaching using educational technology could affect the overall satisfaction. However, since Dr. Jones' department provides complete infrastructural support, he stated he did not experience any conflicts. My question on his turnover intentions elicited more information regarding his job satisfaction.

Yeah, I have a degree in mechanical engineering and so there's lots of opportunities in industry and I've had a number of job offers. I have sort of two contacts. One, through the internships because I run them. So I get to know lots of people in industry. And two, a lot of our students, about half of our students, go into either industry or the big medical research centers, about half go into academia. And so a lot of them get there and say "would you be interested" but I love academia. It's the greatest job in the world, to tell you the truth. Once you get through tenure. Obviously, I mean I've been doing this for 30 years. This university is a nice place to work. Amazing improvement since when I started. Absolutely. ... On well ... I won't get deep into politics but I'm a pretty liberal minded sort of person and it was very very conservative when we first got here. Two, I think the ethnic diversity increased considerably. Still, it's nowhere near where it should be but I love that. Just the differences and cultures and just the strength of the programs. Just our national rankings and lots of different disciplines. Like statistics we're usually in the top 15. ... Absolutely. Pushing towards top 10. So we're one of the top-rated departments in the nation. So those are a lot of the good parts of the job. Plus just the town, it's a nice place to live without the hustle and bustle of the big city where you spend so much of your time just getting to work and back. [cards #82-86 of 90]

C12
D10

Michael Johnston, Interview #7

Dr. Johnston is part of a field that appeared to be growing out of fashion and that phenomenon and the resulting isolation due to peers not being replaced appeared to contribute to his mixed job satisfaction level. Although he has had turnover intentions and is nearing retirement, he seemed to want to remain in academia for the time being.

Well gee that's a loaded question [regarding his job satisfaction]. To be honest with you, of course my situation is unusual. And I am 63 so I could retire, I'll be 64 in August. And I could really retire just about any time. So if I was horribly dissatisfied with what I'm up to, I'd be out of here. On the other hand, I'm part of a discipline that has kind of been defined as being archaic or nonfunctional locally. So the botany program's kind of disappeared. And that's not a satisfying thing. Or, my colleagues when they retire and they move on, they aren't replaced by botanists. So I've kind of gone through an isolation thing, which has its pluses and minuses to be honest with you. ... Well I thought about leaving many times but I never really found a position that would offer me what I have here. And it's a little complicated but the fact is at an institution like this university ... at an institution like this one, you have certain deficiencies academically but because of those deficiencies and the lack of scrutiny, you have a lot of freedom and I've enjoyed that freedom, to be honest with you. [cards #90-97 of 110]

D11   *Carl Andrews, Interview #8*

C14   Dr. Andrews enjoys being a professor, although he finds certain aspects tedious at times. He considers teaching using educational technology and obtaining external research funds just part of the job and those two did not seem to affect his satisfaction level negatively. He did not appear to have turnover intentions. He finds his department culture and collegiality satisfying.

> I enjoy being a professor at the university. It's not always ... when I'm grading finals sometimes ... I get tired of that at times but I think all in all most of us who are here really like, we like teaching, we like doing research, like interacting with interesting people both within and outside the department. Particularly in our area we could all make more money in private industry. ... I have not thought seriously about it [about leaving University A or the professoriate]. ... Well, the more likely would be to go to a different institution but I've been ... maybe early in my career I did but it's been quite a while ago. As long as ... I think the collegiality in this department is really good. If that changed I might consider looking

elsewhere. ... Well, who the department head and his or her expectations, the way the state treats ... the university funding coming into the department. I know that some schools particularly 20 years or so ago some of the schools in the Midwest were having trouble giving raises and they were even taxing departments after the fact. So there were people who left institutions just because it was viewed as though they were never going to get raises and they weren't being rewarded compared to their equals at other institutions. ... I have had colleagues leave for elsewhere for various reasons but and it's often the case that a good professor at a given school, to get them to move elsewhere, the new school has to offer a substantial raise. So in this profession some of the ... there are some people who use that as a way of getting raises. Moving around. I think our department has done a reasonable job of retaining people. [cards #64-71 of 74]

D1   *Lindsay Reeves, Interview #9*

C12   Dr. Reeves stated that she is very satisfied with her job. On the one hand, the experience in teaching using educational technology yields creative satisfaction but on the other hand, the technical problems such as problems with student access are a source of dissatisfaction. She appeared to not have had serious turnover intentions.

Very satisfied. ... I would say ... I was going to say sometimes it depends because I'm really pleased with what I've been able to create, sort of an artistic pleasure. I look at that page and sometimes think gee this is really neat. This sitting up there on the Web, this is my course. On the other hand when students aren't able to access it and there are problems, it's probably a wash. ... When you get done recording and it's all there and with the fade-in music and fade it out, and kind of get this little video, sort of the mini movies. When you see the completed video that's sort of a mini movie, I get a great deal of satisfaction in that. I do. ... I've not thought about leaving the professoriate or academia. I left the practice of law to come into academia because I grew tired of the fighting. And this is my niche in terms of teaching and being able to carry out my role as an advocate but in the teaching realm. In terms of in another position, I would say not recently. Occasionally a job opening will come up and I'll look at it pretty closely and think do I want to move there, looks like a really interesting position. I thought about moving back to the northwest to be closer to family from time to time. And I maybe if the right position were to come open at the right level but right now I have been advancing in a way that I think people that supervise me are trying to make it meaningful and keep me here. [cards #90-94 of 102]

B17   *James Williams, Interview #10*

B19   Dr. Williams is very satisfied with his job. The factors that contribute to his turnover intentions or job stress seem to be related to juggling family and work life and not necessarily from his work life alone. He finds teaching using educational technology compelling enough to invest the extra hours it requires.

I love it here. This is good living. ... This is the best job in the world. I get to do physics all day and I get paid to do it. Man, that's good living. I follow, I get to work on the most interesting questions that be, the university affords me a safe place to go after the most interesting questions about the fundamental universe. The country I live in has enough resources to afford to support me in having students and postdocs and equipment and travel and wonderful colleagues around the country to go ask these questions and go about the business of answering them. It's remarkable. Some of the best and the brightest minds wander around the hall so I could go upstairs and talk to them or down the hall and talk to them. It's remarkably good. I think about the guys I went to college with and they're off in industry, I mean man, my peers are probably making 2, 10, maybe 20 times what I'm making. I don't think ... I make enough so I'm okay there. I don't think I would trade. I'd rather make this much money and get to do what I do than make 20 times as much to do what they do. And let's be real clear. If I could hit a major league curve ball I'd do that instead but I can't. ... I see those as being completely independent. [regarding job satisfaction affected by teaching using educational technology and obtaining external research funds] I am willing to put in extra time in my teaching because I enjoy it, I do not, this is me personally, I don't speak for everybody, I like teaching. I can't stand in a classroom in front of people and for it to be boring. I don't like boring things in my life. And I'm willing to put in 10, 12 hours a lecture to make that lecture be fun. So I put in the extra time and I work very intensely so they're in conflict but I put in enough time so that both get done at a level that I'm happy with. There is conflict, there is no question about it, but I just try to put in enough time such that they're ideal. I mean ... you want to talk about real conflict? The real conflict is I've got two kids at home and a wife on the tenure track which is becoming a much bigger issue. That's what's hard. Spending my time teaching, that's a piece of cake compared to keeping a wife and kids happy and well attended to in some sense. Fifty years ago scientists in my business were wealthy white rich men and they would just spend all their time in a lab and they wouldn't come home. They'd come home or they wouldn't come home. When they came home their wives or the servants had made dinner and they ate and they would go back to the lab. And they would go back to the lab on the weekends and none of them had mistresses and if they ... they would create one that didn't exist so their wives would leave them alone for ... yelling at them for going into the lab so much. That's the hard part. ... Sure. [regarding turnover intentions] All the Yankees think about leaving. All the Yankees are thinking about leaving. There is a culture of ... one of the things that brings all the Yankees together is they talk about how much they hate this place. Okay, that's just the deal. .... Do I think about leaving academia? I don't know. I love it. I'm having an awful lot of fun. Most of the people I revere as they get to their late stages in life or late stages in their career as the funding agencies kind of start to push them out because they want money for the young-er people, you know, think about administrative positions, department head, dean. My wife and I talk about "Hey, let's go to Wellesley. Wouldn't it be great, we'll go teach at Wellesley, wouldn't that be a wonderful thing?" It would be fun for about a semester or two. Or, we'll go back home and work on Wall Street and get rich but that's not .... Look, if they came calling for her and they could find a position for me, I'll go. I'm content. The thing that makes me think about leaving is not the teaching or the lack of support for the teaching. [cards #92-107 of 110]

B19   **Summary of Findings**

The purpose of this interpretive critical inquiry included com-ing to understand the experience of faculty at public research universities who teach using educational technology and their perception of how the demands of two apparently conflict-ing requirements—teaching using educational technology and obtaining external research funds—affect their job sat-isfaction as professors. Three research questions were asked to guide me in coming to understand the faculty experience. The research questions were: (a) What is the experience of faculty members who teach using educational technology at a public research university? (b) How is the experience affecting them as more demands are placed on faculty to obtain exter-nal research funds? and (c) How is the experience affecting their job satisfaction? In this chapter, based on the themes and subthemes that emerged as a result of analyzing the interview data, answers were provided to the three research questions as findings. This section summarizes the findings for each research question.

B5   *Research Question 1.*
      What is the experience of faculty members who teach using educational technology at a public research university?

The participants used educational technology to teach in a variety of ways with different goals or motivations in mind. Some pedagogical goals included increasing learner-learner interactions and providing opportunities for students to actively listen and absorb the lectures instead of focusing on taking down the copious amounts of notes. Still some used it to supplement their face-to-face courses while others used it to teach online courses or deliver distance education. The tools they used ranged from PowerPoint slides, to audio and video clips, and to asynchronous discussion boards.

B2   The participants appeared to find the experience of teaching using educational technology personally rewarding. They seemed to enjoy the creative outcomes as well as a sense of service in delivering higher education to remote students who otherwise would not have been able to participate in higher learning. Some thought teaching using educational technology afforded pedagogical improvements as well as flexibility and convenience for the students and themselves.

A9   However, they appeared to encounter a variety of barriers that included time constraints, steep learning curves, technical problems, and pedagogical challenges. Strong institutional and departmental infrastructural support appeared to alleviate some of the barriers. The participants who seemed least challenged by teaching—meaning, who experienced fewer barriers—using educational technology seemed to be those with the most infrastructural support.

B7   *Research Question 2.*

B9   *How is the experience affecting them as more demands are placed on faculty to obtain external research funds?*

A participant's work life as a faculty member in a research university appeared to be characterized by autonomy and independence but with clear expectations to be conducting research that is externally funded, the most important reward criterion. Thus in the light of this distinct reward criterion, the autonomy attribute seemed to become conditional autonomy; faculty appeared to be autonomous as long as they were productive awardees of external research funds. The second or third criterion appeared to be teaching. Thus, among the triumvirate research university's mission of research, teaching, and service, clearly funded research rested at the apex followed by service and teaching at the base. Please see Figure 4 on page 173. The participants also portrayed a work life exemplified by constant juggling of tasks, which appeared to be a source of job dissatisfaction.

B5   Of the externally funded grants, those with higher indirect costs appeared to be preferred by the administration and these fees seemed to be used to augment a department's, college's, or institution's operating budget. The participants also spoke of how the funds awarded to them via grants were used: to support their summer salaries, to help build their research programs, and to fund their graduate and post doctoral students.

B9   Because obtaining external research funds appeared to be very competitive with a low success rate, participants shared different strategies they have used or intended to use to be successful awardees. Some stated they conducted research in areas where funding was more readily available and some collaborated with other faculty members at their institution or elsewhere. Some participants also shared their intentions to explore opportunities to conduct educational research. However, conducting educational research appeared to be out of the ordinary for participants in the science fields.

B11   *Research Question 3.*
       How is the experience affecting their job satisfaction?

Surprisingly, a majority of the participants appeared to be satisfied with their positions at either University A or University B. Many of them shared that the professoriate is an ideal job. However, all of them had turnover intentions at one time or another although only two had recent turnover intentions. The reasons behind the turnover intentions appeared to be both personal and professional. The personal reasons appeared to include an opportunity to move closer to their extended families. The professional reasons appeared to include a strategy for salary increase. Teaching using educational technology for many appeared to add to their job satisfaction.

Appendix

Missions Of A Research University

As academics (one retired and now deceased) interested in the effect that a constructivist posture might have on the mission of a research-oriented university, we have devised the following brief outline describing what the mission statement of such a university might encompass. What we tried to do was to imagine how a university might organize itself around teaching, research, and service if most of its academic faculty shared a constructivist paradigm, rather like earlier research universities which shared a positivist paradigm. How would most faculty utilize their time? What kinds of public service activities might they engage in? How would they teach differently? Toward what kinds of inquiries would their research efforts be directed? How would they re-frame graduate teaching and mentoring? What might the overall university mission statement look like?

Clearly, no such place will likely ever exist. Much more likely is that universities will begin to accommodate multiple paradigms of inquiry much as they are accommodating diversity in their student ranks and increasing diversity in their faculty ranks. But it was an interesting exercise, and we share it with readers in the hopes that others may

The Constructivist Credo, by Yvonna S. Lincoln and Egon G. Guba. 199–201
© 2013 Left Coast Press, Inc. All rights reserved.

experiment with writing models for universities based on very different paradigms and lenses(for example, critical theory, feminist theory, race/ethnic theories) in order to reflect what different forms universities might take in their ongoing differentiation. Such *gedankenexperimente*, "thought experiments," are not unuseful, since universities and their missions are now "up for grabs" in an era of academic capitalism and the marketing of "distinctiveness" within the higher education organizational ecology. Needless to say, this statement below is based specifically on constructivism; other paradigms require different statements, and permit very different outcomes.

1. Research universities have three general missions: research, teaching, and service.

2. Such a university's research mission is to conduct inquiry and to promulgate the results of that inquiry in the form of local theorizing—sets of working hypotheses that are locally applicable and adaptable.

3. Such a university's teaching mission is threefold:

   a. To provide a basic but broad-ranging undergraduate program which has as a major (but not sole) priority the development of a recruitment pool for its own and other research universities' graduate programs.

   b. To create inquiry colleagues—researchers who are competent to become colleagues of their mentors and of similar others at comparable institutions—trained at the graduate level; to reproduce itself (CAVEAT: being certain to introduce new "genetic" material with high frequency).

   c. To create practitioner colleagues—practitioners oriented to the dual tasks of grounding and testing theories locally, trained at both graduate and undergraduate levels and tempered in the crucible of local settings.

4. Such a university's service function is likewise threefold:

   a. To elicit inputs from practitioner colleagues that will provide stimulation and grounding for future theoretical developments.

    b. To test already developed theories in those arenas in which they have been grounded, that is, locally, and in full and interactive partnership with practitioner colleagues.

    c. To be open to problems and questions posed by practitioner colleagues and to respond to them in the spirit of mutual interest.

5. In their work of theory development, university researchers and their practitioner colleagues should keep the following criteria for theories foremost in mind:

    a. That theory is most useful which lends itself most easily to meaningful local adaptations.

    b. That theory is most successful that both improves professional practice and is informed by that practice, that is, that fits, that works, that has local relevance, and that is open to reconstruction as new information and more sophisticated modes of analysis and interpretation become available.

References

Arendt, H. (2008). Truth and politics. In J. Medina & D. Wood (Eds.), *Truth: Engagements across philosophical traditions* (pp. 295–314). Ames, IA: Blackwell.

Baez, B., & Boyles, D. (2009). *The politics of inquiry: Education research and the "Culture of Science."* Albany: State University of New York Press.

Bleier, R. (1988). *Feminist approaches to science.* Oxford: Pergamon Press.

Bravo-Moreno, A. (2003). Power games between the researcher and the participant. *The Qualitative Report, 8*(4), 624–639.

Cannella, G., and Lincoln, Y. S. (2004). Dangerous discourses: Epilogue: Claiming a critical public social science—reconceptualizing and redeploying research. *Qualitative Inquiry, 10*(2), 298–309.

Ceglowski, D. (2000). Research as relationship. *Qualitative Inquiry, 6*(1), 88–103.

Charmaz, K. (2008). Grounded theory as an emergent method. In S. N. Hesse-Biber & P. Leavy (Eds.), *Handbook of emergent methods* (pp. 155–172). New York: Guilford Press.

Collins, M., Shattel, M., & Thomas, S. P. (2005). Problematic interviewee behaviors in qualitative research. *Western Journal of Nursing Research, 27*(2), 188–199.

Duncombe, J., & Jessop, J. (2002). "Doing rapport" and the ethics of "faking friendship." In M. Muthner, N. Birch, J. Jessop, & T. Miller (Eds.), *Ethics in qualitative research* (pp. 107–122). London: Sage.

Ebbs, C. A. (1996). Qualitative research inquiry: Issues of power and ethics. *Education, 117*(2), 217–222.

Eisner, E. (1993). Forms of Understanding and the Future of Educational Research. Presidential Address, American Educational Research Association Annual Meeting, Atlanta, Georgia, April, 1993.

Faubion, J. D., & Marcus, G. E. (Eds.). (2009). *Fieldwork is not what it used to be: Learning anthropology's method in a time of transition.* Ithaca, NY: Cornell University Press.

Gage, N. L. (1989). The paradigm wars and their aftermath: A historical sketch of research on teaching. *Educational Researcher, 18*(7), 4–10.

Gould, S. J. (1993). *Eight little piggies: Reflection in natural history.* New York: W.W. Norton.

Guba, E. G., & Lincoln, Y. S. (1981). *Effective evaluation: Improving the usefulness of evaluation results through responsive and naturalistic approaches.* San Francisco: Jossey-Bass.

Guba, E. G., & Lincoln, Y. S. (1989). *Fourth generation evaluation.* Thousand Oaks, CA: Sage.

Kahn, J. P., Mastrioanni, A. C., & Sugarman, J. (1998). Changing claims about justice in research: An introduction and overview. In J. P. Kahn, A. C. Mastrioanni, & J. Sugarman (Eds.), *Beyond consent: Seeking justice in research* (pp. 1–10). New York: Oxford University Press.

Karnieli-Miller, O., Strier, R., & Pessach, L. (2009). Power relations in qualitative research. *Qualitative Health Research, 19*(2), 279–289.

Knorr-Cetina, K., & Mulkay, J. (1983). *Science observed: Perspectives on the social study of science.* London: Sage.

Kosko, B. (1993). *Fuzzy thinking: The new science of fuzzy logic.* New York: Hyperion.

Kuhn, T. (1967). *The structure of scientific revolutions.* Chicago: University of Chicago Press.

Lincoln, Y. S. (1993). Emergent Paradigms and the Crisis in Psychology. Keynote Address, Inter-American Congress of Psychology Annual Meeting, Santiago, Chile.

Lincoln, Y. S., and Cannella, G. (2004). Qualitative research, power, and the radical right. *Qualitative Inquiry, 10*(2), 175–201.

Lincoln, Y. S., & Cannella, G. (2009). Ethics and the broader rethinking/reconceptualization of research as construct. *Cultural Studies ⟷ Critical Methodologies, 9*(2), 124–137.

Lincoln, Y. S., & Denzin, N. K. (2005). Epilogue: The eighth and ninth moments—Qualitative research in/and the fractured future. In N. K. Denzin and Y. S. Lincoln (Eds.), *The SAGE handbook of qualitative research* (3rd ed., pp. 1115–1126). Thousand Oaks, CA: Sage.

Lincoln, Y. S., & Denzin, N. K. (2011). Epilogue: Toward a "Refunctioned Ethnography." In N. K. Denzin & Y. S. Lincoln (Eds.), *The SAGE handbook of qualitative research,* (4th ed., pp. 715–718). Thousand Oaks, CA: Sage.

Lincoln, Y. S., & Guba, E. G. (1985). *Naturalistic inquiry.* Thousand Oaks, CA: Sage.

Lincoln, Y. S., & Guba, E. G. (1986). Research, evaluation and policy analysis: Heuristics for disciplined inquiry. *Policy Studies Review, 5*(3), 546–565.

Lincoln, Y. S., and Tierney, W. G. (2004). Qualitative research and institutional review boards (IRBs). *Qualitative Inquiry, 10*(2), 219–234.

Namenwirth, M. (1988). Science seen through a feminist prism. In R. Bleier (Ed.), *Feminist approaches to science* (pp. 18–41). Oxford: Pergamon Press.

National Research Council. (2002). *Scientific research in education.* Committee on Scientific Principles for Education Research. R. J. Shavelson& L. Towne, Eds. Center for Education. Division of Behavioral and Social Sciences and Education. Washington, DC: National Academy Press.

O'Connor, D. L., & O'Neill, B. J. (2004). Toward social justice: Teaching qualitative research. *Journal of Teaching in Social Work, 24*(3/4), 19–33.

Reason, P. (1994). *Participation in human inquiry.* London: Sage.

Schwandt, T. A. (19). Farewell to criteriology. *Qualitative Inquiry, 2*(1), 58–72.

Strier, R. (2007). Anti-oppressive research in social work: A preliminary definition. *British Journal of Social Work, 37*(5), 857–871.

Westbrook, D. A. (2008). *Navigators of the contemporary: Why ethnography matters.* Chicago: University of Chicago Press.

About the Authors

Yvonna S. Lincoln is Ruth Harrington Chair of Educational Leadership and University Distinguished Professor of Higher Education at Texas A&M University, where she also serves as Program Chair for the higher education program area. She is the co-editor, with Norman K. Denzin, of the journal *Qualitative Inquiry,* and of the 1st, 2nd, 3rd and 4th editions of the *Sage Handbook of Qualitative Research,* and the *Handbook of Critical and Indigenous Methodologies.* As well, she is or has been the co-author, editor or co-editor of more than a half dozen other books and volumes, including *Effective Evaluation, Naturalistic Inquiry ,* and *Fourth Generation Evaluation,* all with Egon Guba (her late spouse), and *Organization Theory and Inquiry.* She has served as the President of the Association for the Study of Higher Education and of the American Evaluation Association, and as the Vice President for Division J (Postsecondary Education) for the American Educational Research Association. She is the author or co-author of more than 100 chapters and journal articles on aspects of higher education or qualitative research methods and methodologies. She is the winner of the Sidney Suslow Award, the Lazarsfeld Award for Evaluation Research, and the Howard Bowen Award for lifetime contributions to the profession of higher education. She was also awarded the Lifetime Achievement Award from the International Congress of Qualitative Inquiry in 2010. Her research interests include development of qualitative methods and methodologies, the status and future of research libraries, and other issues in higher education. She currently writes an occasional column for the higher education blog, www.21stcenturyscholar.com, where she comments on the rapidly-evolving status of research universities in the United States.

The late **Egon G. Guba** (1924–2008) was a major figure in educational research and theory, and program evaluation. He was a leading proponent of constructivism within the social sciences. Trained as a quantitative researcher at University of Chicago, he taught at the University of Chicago, University of Kansas City, and the Ohio State University, followed by twenty-three years at Indiana University, Bloomington, from which he retired in 1989. His work on constructivism was developed over the span of several decades, including groundbreaking books coauthored with Yvonna S. Lincoln.